Ruth Mott's
FAVOURITE RECIPES

Ruth Mott's
FAVOURITE RECIPES

Ruth Mott

WITH WENDY HOBSON

BBC BOOKS

For BERTHA *and* EDNA
and with thanks to LADY ILIFFE *for her invaluable help*
and all the people throughout my lifetime
who have helped me on my way.

Food photography and photographs of Ruth Mott by Tim Imrie. All other photographs reproduced by kind permission of Ruth Mott from her personal album.

The author and publishers would like to thank John Tovey for his kind permission to reproduce the recipe on page 201. This originally appeared in Entertaining with Tovey, *published by Macdonald General Books, 1979.*

The recipe on page 200 is adapted from The Farmhouse Kitchen Baking Book *by Grace Mulligan published by William Collins Sons & Co Ltd, 1988, in association with Yorkshire Television Enterprises Ltd, © Yorkshire Television Ltd and reproduced by kind permission.*

Published by BBC Books
A division of BBC Enterprises Limited
Woodlands, 80 Wood Lane
London W12 0TT

First published 1990
Reprinted 1990
Copyright © 1990 Ruth Mott

ISBN 0 563 36039 9

Typeset in 11/13 Garamond
Printed and bound in Great Britain by Butler & Tanner Ltd, Frome
Jacket printed by Belmont Press, Northampton

CONTENTS

INTRODUCTION

I love cooking, and I have many people to thank who gave me such an interest in cooking and made it my life, especially my mother.

My view of cookery has been gleaned from years of working as a cook in big houses. I don't see myself as a professional cook, though, but someone who really loves cooking and has learnt by experience. If you say you are a professional cook, people think nothing should ever go wrong, but it does go wrong for everyone from time to time!

My ideas have moderated quite a bit over the years as things changed. In the old days, there was only 'cream' just as it came from the farm; now you can choose from shelves of different types! And I do like to try all the new things and keep up to date with what is available.

Lifestyles change too. Nowadays we are warned of the dangers of too much fat in our diet so we use less butter and fats. Whereas my father was a wonderful advert for fatty food – four meals a day, with lots of butter and home-cured bacon with plenty of fat – he worked hard but he lived a healthy life. In fact, most of the country folk ate the same, but they all worked long hours and very hard, at work and at home, whereas now we don't do the tough manual work to compensate for that diet. But we always had plenty of vegetables and fruit, too, grown in the garden round the house or on the allotment, and everything was home-made so we kept a balance in our diet.

I still use quite a lot of butter and cream in my cooking, and no doubt I will be drummed out by the health food people, but I learnt to cook before 'health diets' became a way of life. And I don't eat these things all the time. If you ate eggs, chips and beefburgers every day it would probably give you ulcers. But provided you are sensible, there is no reason why you should not use cream now and then, or bake the odd treacle pudding.

I have tried to include recipes for all occasions; something everyone can afford and will understand with no complicated methods or fancy terms. There are plenty of everyday dishes, snacks and puddings plus some wonderful recipes for the best dinner parties.

For any recipes, I am always looking for short cuts and quick ways to do things. I learnt very young in service that you had to keep your wits about you and learn from your own and other people's experience. Once you lost your afternoon off redoing something from scratch, you soon remembered how it should be done. So I have tried to pass on some of the tips I use – most of which you won't find in any cookery manuals because they are my naughty ways of doing things!

I think that if you need to save time and can find short cuts – use them. This is not a cookery book for the purists. I am not against using whatever products you choose which make life easier for you. After all, we lead busy lives these days and time is precious. I always keep some frozen puff pastry in the freezer and a tin of beef consommé in the cupboard plus some red and white wine. If you don't have the time or the inclination to make your own mayonnaise or salad dressings, there are plenty of good brands in the supermarket for you to choose from. We all have to use prepared stuff sometimes – and why not?

There are plenty of other things I keep in my cupboards and freezer, too, so that I can always put an interesting dish together. You should never be afraid to use what you have in the store cupboard and vary the recipes to suit yourself. If you do not like a particular ingredient, leave it out and use something else. You can adapt most things, and with a little practice you soon get to know how to create your own recipes using other people's ideas.

One of the best ways to learn is by tasting. It sounds obvious, but it is vital to keep tasting as you cook so that you know what to expect, and what to add if you feel your dish needs a little extra zip.

I enjoy my cooking. I hope you enjoy sharing some of my favourite recipes with me.

NOTES ON THE RECIPES
Most of the recipes serve 4, unless otherwise marked.
Spoon measurements are level.
Do not mix imperial and metric measurements: follow one set only.
Eggs are size 2.

Part One

APPETISERS

Beignets Soufflés Fromage

[SERVES 4]

These delicious choux pastry puffs make a lovely starter, or you can cook them without the mustard and cheese and serve them with cream and apricot jam for a dessert. I always use a kitchen thermometer to make sure that the frying oil is not too hot – 325°F (160°C) is about right – otherwise they will turn into hard knobs. If the temperature is right, they will cook slowly, puff up and turn themselves over in the pan. You can then turn up the heat to brown them. Lift them out of the pan with a slotted spoon to shake off the fat.

3¾ oz (95 g) plain flour

1 teaspoon mustard powder

salt and freshly ground black pepper

7 fl oz (200 ml) water

3 oz (75 g) unsalted butter

3 eggs, beaten

2 oz (50 g) Parmesan cheese, grated

oil for deep frying

Mix together the flour and mustard and season with salt and freshly ground black pepper. Place the water and butter in a saucepan and cook over a low heat until the butter has melted. Raise the heat and rapidly bring the mixture to the boil. Take the pan off the heat and add the flour. Mix in quickly with a wooden spoon, then beat just until the dough is smooth and comes away from the sides of the pan. Allow the mixture to cool slightly, then beat in the eggs, a little at a time, followed by the grated cheese. Heat the frying oil to 325°F (160°C), then deep fry dessertspoonsful of the choux pastry in batches for about 7 to 10 minutes. Turn the heat up to 338°F (170°C) for the last minute until they are crisp and golden brown. Keep them warm while frying the remaining beignets.

Unsalted butter is more expensive, but gives the best taste to any recipe; I always use it. You can add salt to a recipe if you like, but once there you can't take it out.

Potato Surprises

[SERVES 4]

Children love this delicious and simple dish. We often used to serve it for nursery lunches. Then we could be sure that the children had eaten a substantial starter, even if they did not like one of the first courses served to the adults.

4 large baking potatoes, scrubbed

2 oz (50 g) unsalted butter

2 tablespoons milk

salt and freshly ground black pepper

4 eggs

4 tablespoons single cream

Pre-heat the oven to 350°F (180°C), gas mark 4. Cut an oval-shaped slice in the skin on the top of each potato without removing any of the skin. Bake for about 1½ hours until tender.

Remove the potatoes from the oven. Carefully slice off the tops and scrape out most of the insides with a teaspoon. Place the potato skins on a baking dish. Mash the potato flesh with the butter and milk and season to taste with salt and freshly ground black pepper. Break an egg into each potato skin and spoon over the cream. Pipe the mashed potato round the top edge of the potato skins and return them to the oven for about 15 to 20 minutes until the eggs are cooked to your liking. The cream will help to keep the yolks soft.

Jerusalem Artichokes in Curry Sauce

[SERVES 4]

This dish can also be made in exactly the same way using leeks instead of Jerusalem artichokes, or replacing the Curry Sauce with a Béchamel Sauce (see page 194).

1 lb (450 g) Jerusalem artichokes

1 pint (600 ml) Curry Sauce (see page 193)

4 oz (100 g) Cheddar cheese, grated

Scrub and peel the artichokes. Place them in boiling salted water and boil for about 15 to 20 minutes until nearly cooked. Remove carefully on to a cloth to drain.

Meanwhile, make the curry sauce. Pre-heat the oven 375°F (190°C), gas mark 5. Pour some of the sauce into a gratin dish, add the vegetables, then cover with the remaining sauce. Sprinkle on the grated cheese and finish off the dish in the oven for about 15 to 20 minutes until the top is brown and bubbling.

Mushroom Tartlets

[SERVES 4]

I like to make my own shortcrust pastry with plenty of butter for a nice crispy pastry for filling, but you can use a proprietary brand if you need to save time.

I don't reckon to waste anything, and this is a particularly good recipe for using up left-overs and adapting to what you like to use. You can vary the ingredients, adding ham, tongue or cooked chicken, or include other vegetables such as peppers. You can even use the pastry left over when you have made pie or flan.

8 oz (225 g) Shortcrust Pastry (see page 199)

1 tablespoon oil

1 medium onion, chopped

2 rashers bacon, finely chopped

8 oz (225 g) mushrooms, sliced

½ pint (300 ml) Béchamel Sauce (see page 194)

chopped fresh parsley to garnish

Pre-heat the oven to 400°F (200°C), gas mark 6. Roll out the pastry and use it to line 12 bun tins. Prick the pastry with a fork, line with greaseproof paper and fill with ceramic or dried beans. Bake for about 10 minutes, remove the greaseproof paper and beans, then bake for a further 5 minutes until the pastry is dry and lightly browned.

Meanwhile, heat the oil and fry the onion for about 5 minutes until transparent. Add the bacon and mushrooms and fry for about 4 minutes until cooked. Make the béchamel sauce and add the cooked ingredients. When the tart cases are ready, turn down the oven to 350°F (180°C), gas mark 4. Fill the cases and return them to the oven for about 10 minutes to heat through. Sprinkle with chopped parsley to serve.

Chicory in a Blanket

[SERVES 4]

As well as a tasty appetiser, this dish makes a good lunch dish and is ideal for vegetarians if you leave out the ham. You can substitute leeks for the chicory if you prefer.

4 heads chicory, trimmed

4 slices ham

1 pint (600 ml) Cheese Sauce (see page 192)

2 oz (50 g) Parmesan cheese, grated

Place the chicory heads in a pan of salted water, bring to the boil, and boil for about 15 to 20 minutes, handling them carefully so they keep their shape. Or you can steam them for about 25 minutes. Drain well. Pre-heat the oven to 400°F (200°C), gas mark 6. Wrap each chicory head in a slice of ham and place them in a gratin dish. Cover with the cheese sauce, sprinkle on the Parmesan and place in the oven for about 15 minutes to heat through until the top is a nice golden brown.

HERBS FROM THE GARDEN

I never use dried herbs, except perhaps oregano or something like that, because I grow them in the garden. There's such a difference in the taste that it is worth using fresh herbs if you possibly can. Even if you don't grow your own, you can buy them in all supermarkets now. You get used to which ones to use in moderation as some, such as rosemary and thyme, are very strong.

I always grow plenty of parsley, because I use more of that than anything. Mint either likes you or it doesn't. Mine rampages over the garden so I plant it in an old sink from a building site to contain it. Chives are delicious on a potato salad, and I usually grow thyme, sage and dill. I have a rosemary bush and a little bay tree, which is always losing its leaves! I also have a lovely tarragon bush which I brought from France, slightly different from the tarragon you get here.

I have grown garlic, but it only makes tiny little things and I like a big clove. I used to bring strings back from France, which were wonderful. I don't grow many vegetables now, although I do have a couple of gro-bags for some tomatoes and runner beans, and sometimes plant a few courgettes as they will grow anywhere.

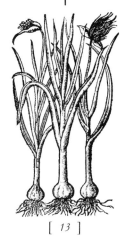

Tomato Cups with Asparagus

[SERVES 4]

Tomatoes make wonderful appetisers. Not only do they whet the appetite without being too filling, they can so quickly be brought into use. This is another dish which can be varied depending on what you have left over in the fridge, but it looks lovely if carefully arranged and presented on the plate. Use a good quality mayonnaise if you don't want to make your own.

---

8 large tomatoes

---

2 oz (50 g) cooked peas

---

2 oz (50 g) cooked asparagus tips

---

4 fl oz (120 ml) Creamy Mayonnaise (see page 197)

---

salt and freshly ground black pepper

---

4 thin slices wholemeal bread, crusts removed

---

2 oz (50 g) unsalted butter

---

4 sprigs of fresh parsley to garnish

Cut a thin slice from the top of each tomato and remove the seeds. Mix the peas and asparagus tips into the mayonnaise and season to taste with salt and freshly ground black pepper. Pile the mixture back into the tomatoes and replace the lids at a jaunty angle. Spread the bread with the butter and carefully roll the slices lengthways like a bread Swiss roll. Slice each roll into four rounds and arrange the tomatoes and bread on individual plates. Garnish with the sprigs of parsley.

I worked in lots of big houses as a young woman because I needed to be quite near to home. My mother was crippled with rheumatoid arthritis, and I took temporary jobs so that I could come home every few weeks and go through the house to give it a thorough clean. Or I took jobs near home so that I could come home on my half day. Of course, all the kitchen staff lived in, so there were no 'day jobs' and you did not finish until all the work was done. In those days I earned £1. 3s. 4d. a month, and even the butler only earned between £3 and £5 a week!

These days, big houses are lucky to be able to find staff who will live in if they can afford it at all, since the employer provides not only wages, but housing and food as well. The old landed gentry are no longer those with the money since their properties cost so much to keep up. Their old investments in shipping, railways and tobacco were the source of a stable income, whereas now share prices go up and down, and they may have money today and none tomorrow.

Garlic Baked Tomatoes

[SERVES 4]

This makes a simple and delicious starter, with the breadcrumbs softened inside by the tomato flesh and crisped on top by the drop of oil. Walnut oil gives a nice flavour, but you can use any cooking oil, and substitute pesto sauce for the basil, if you wish, but use only $\frac{1}{4}$ teaspoon as it is very concentrated.

Basil should always be used sparingly as it has a strong flavour. Once a month I visit a friend and we take it in turns to prepare supper. On one occasion, he added a bit more basil to the turkey because it did not look much on the plate, so we ended up eating basil sandwiches!

4 large tomatoes
1 small clove garlic, finely chopped
$\frac{1}{2}$ teaspoon chopped fresh basil
1 teaspoon chopped fresh parsley
2 oz (50 g) fresh breadcrumbs
salt and freshly ground black pepper
$1\frac{1}{2}$ tablespoons walnut oil

Slice off the top of each tomato and carefully remove the pips and membrane with a teaspoon. Turn the tomatoes upside down to drain. Mix the tomato flesh with the garlic, basil, parsley and breadcrumbs. Season to taste with salt and freshly ground black pepper, then return the mixture to the tomato cases. Dribble a little oil on top of each tomato. Place under the grill for a few minutes until the tomatoes are heated through and the top is beginning to crisp.

Hot Grapefruit Soufflés

[SERVES 4]

It is so much easier and more enjoyable to eat a grapefruit which is properly prepared. It takes a little extra trouble, but it is well worth the effort. Ladies used to say they always liked eating my grapefruit because they were no trouble; with everybody else's they had to struggle!

2 large grapefruit

2 eggs, separated

2 oz (50 g) sugar

Pre-heat the oven to 425 °F (220 °C), gas mark 7. Slice the grapefruit in half crossways. It is easiest to use a curved serrated grapefruit knife to prepare the fruit, but a small bladed knife will do. Cut down each side of the membrane and through the skin at the top, flicking out any pips as you go. Gently hold on to the core and lift out the centre of the grapefruit, letting the segments fall back into place. Then cut round the edge. Place the grapefruit in the oven to heat through while you prepare the topping.

Beat the egg yolks with $\frac{1}{2}$ oz (15 g) sugar until pale yellow. Whisk the whites until stiff, then fold in the remaining sugar. Carefully fold the whites into the yolks. Cover the grapefruit halves with the egg mixture and return to the hot oven, or place under the grill for about 2 minutes until golden brown.

Eggs Mollets

[SERVES 4]

You must use eggs which are at least three days old for this recipe, otherwise they are too difficult to shell while they are warm and soft. This is not too much of a problem now, but we used to have to remember not to use the eggs we had just collected from the local farm.

4 eggs

$\frac{1}{2}$ pint (300 ml) Béchamel Sauce (see page 194)
or Curry Sauce (see page 193)
or Cheese Sauce (see page 192)

Place the eggs in a saucepan of boiling water and boil for 6 to 7 minutes. While they are cooking, prepare your chosen sauce. Plunge the cooked eggs into a basin of cold water, then tap all round the eggs and carefully remove the shells. Drop the shelled eggs in a basin of warm water to keep them soft while you shell the remaining eggs and complete the sauce. Place the eggs in a gratin dish, cover with the sauce and serve at once.

Egg and Tuna Mousse

[SERVES 4]

Recipes which you can prepare in advance are often a good idea when you are entertaining as you can spend your time with the guests and not in the kitchen. This is a very light mousse, but it has plenty of flavour.

1 × 6 ½ oz (185 g) tin tuna fish, drained and flaked

4 hard-boiled eggs, finely chopped

2 tomatoes, skinned and finely chopped
or 1 × 8 oz (225 g) tin tomatoes, finely chopped

salt and freshly ground black pepper

1 tablespoon chopped fresh chives

1 tablespoon chopped fresh parsley

1 teaspoon anchovy essence

2 drops Worcestershire sauce

1 × 15 oz (425 g) tin beef consommé

2 teaspoons gelatine powder

¼ pint (150 ml) double cream, lightly whipped

½ cucumber, diced

Mix the flaked fish with the finely chopped eggs and tomatoes. Season to taste with salt and freshly ground black pepper and mix in the chives, parsley, anchovy essence and Worcestershire sauce. Do not mash the mixture; the final result should be coarse. Heat the consommé in a saucepan, sprinkle on the gelatine and stir to dissolve. Allow to cool. Stir the consommé into the fish mixture when beginning to set, then fold in the lightly whipped cream. Pour into a 2 pint (1.2 litre) soufflé dish and refrigerate for about 2 hours until set. Cover the top with the diced cucumber and serve with wholemeal bread and butter.

It is so important to taste your cooking the whole time, checking to make sure that it is how you like it. If I find it is not quite what I want, I go to the cupboard and see what I have which will give it a bit of zip. Worcestershire sauce is a grand thing – I shake it into lots of dishes and it usually does the trick. A dash of sherry is also a great standby.

Oeufs Basildon

Illustrated on page 34

[SERVES 4 TO 6]

This recipe is named after Basildon Park, the home of Lord and Lady Iliffe. I served it there on many occasions and it was always popular. For a change, you can omit the taramasalata and flavour the egg and mayonnaise mixture with a little mustard or some finely chopped ham.

6 hard-boiled eggs

1 oz (25 g) unsalted butter

½ pint (300 ml) Creamy Mayonnaise (see page 197)

2 oz (50 g) Taramasalata (see page 20)

salt and freshly ground black pepper

2 bunches of watercress, washed

10 lettuce leaves, washed

Cut the eggs in half lengthways, remove the yolks and rub them through a fine sieve. Soften the butter and work in the egg yolks and 1 dessertspoon of mayonnaise. Mix in the taramasalata and season to taste with salt and freshly ground black pepper. Pile the mixture back into the egg whites and reshape. Boil 1 bunch of watercress in salted water for 5 minutes. Drain and chop finely. Mix it into the remaining mayonnaise. Arrange the lettuce leaves on a serving dish with the eggs on top. Coat with the green mayonnaise and garnish with the remaining watercress.

Oeufs à L'Indienne

[SERVES 4]

I always use freshly ground black pepper. Once you have tried it, you never go back to ready ground white pepper; it just does not have the taste. Some people prefer to use white peppercorns in mayonnaise to avoid having black specks, but I think the taste more than makes up for that. It is hard to imagine how we coped without peppercorns years ago!

4 hard-boiled eggs

1 tablespoon chopped fresh chives

salt and freshly ground black pepper

½ lettuce, washed

FOR THE SAUCE:

4 tablespoons double cream, lightly whipped

2 teaspoons Madras curry powder or paste

½ teaspoon ginger

1 tablespoon mango chutney purée

1 tablespoon apricot jam

Cut the eggs in half lengthways. Remove the yolks and press them through a sieve. Mix the yolks with the chives and season to taste with salt and freshly ground black pepper. Pile the mixture back into the whites and arrange them on a bed of lettuce leaves. Mix together the sauce ingredients, pour over the eggs and serve.

Egg and Spinach Tart

[SERVES 4]

This tart needs to be eaten as soon as it is cooked, so make sure your diners are ready before you finish making it.

8 oz (225 g) Shortcrust Pastry (see page 199)

1 lb (450 g) spinach, washed

3 oz (75 g) unsalted butter

4 tablespoons single cream

salt and freshly ground black pepper

a pinch of nutmeg

6 eggs, beaten

Pre-heat the oven to 400°F (200°C), gas mark 6. Use the pastry to line an 8 in (20 cm) flan tin. Prick all over with a fork, cover with greaseproof paper and ceramic or dried beans and bake blind for about 15 minutes. Remove the greaseproof paper and beans and bake for a further 5 to 10 minutes until the pastry is dry and lightly browned.

Meanwhile, place the washed spinach in a saucepan, without extra water, cover and cook gently for about 10 minutes. Drain, then either chop finely or process until smooth. Mix in 1 oz (25 g) of the butter and the cream, and season to taste with salt, freshly ground black pepper and a pinch of nutmeg. Spread in the flan case and keep it warm.

Season the beaten eggs with salt and freshly ground black pepper. Melt 1 oz (25 g) of the butter in a large saucepan. Add the eggs and cook over a gentle heat, stirring continuously, until they are cooked, but still nice and moist. Remove from the heat and stir in the remaining butter. This keeps the egg soft and makes it shiny. Cover the flan case with the scrambled egg and serve at once.

Taramasalata

[SERVES 4]

You can serve taramasalata with toast as an appetiser, or with crusty bread and salad as a more substantial lunch dish. It can also be used in the recipe for Oeufs Basildon (see page 18).

8 oz (225 g) smoked cod roe, skinned and chopped

6 tablespoons olive oil

a squeeze of lemon juice

1 tablespoon single cream

1 clove garlic, finely chopped

Mix the cod roe with 2 tablespoons of oil and leave to soften for about 1 hour. Add the remaining ingredients and process or pass through a fine sieve until smooth.

Try adding fromage frais to your savoury recipes instead of cream. Apart from having less fat, it can taste nicer than cream in savoury dishes because it has a sharper flavour. Always remember not to boil it, though, as it tends to separate.

Smoked Mackerel or Kipper Pâté

[SERVES 4]

A pâté is always a popular starter, and a fish pâté can be a little lighter than one made with meat. Use unsalted or clarified butter to seal the pâté and make it look attractive. This freezes well so you can prepare it in advance, or make twice the quantity, use one straight away and freeze one for later.

4 smoked mackerel or kipper fillets

4 oz (100 g) unsalted butter, melted

1 tablespoon natural yoghurt, fromage frais or double cream

1 tablespoon lemon juice

salt and freshly ground black pepper

2 tomatoes, sliced

4 sprigs of watercress

Remove any skin and bones from the fish and place the flesh in the food processor. Add 1 oz (25 g) melted butter and the yoghurt, fromage frais or cream, whichever you prefer. Process the mixture until it is nice and smooth. Mix in about 1 tablespoon lemon juice, or to taste, and season with salt and freshly ground black pepper. Turn into a pâté dish and refrigerate for about 2 hours until firm. Then cover with the remaining melted butter. Garnish with the tomato and watercress, and serve with buttered brown bread and a green salad.

Mock Caviare Soufflé

[SERVES 4]

This recipe dates back to 1880. It makes a tasty appetiser when you are entertaining as it can be prepared in advance.

2 teaspoons gelatine

1 tablespoon water

2 tablespoons Creamy Mayonnaise (see page 197)

2 tablespoons lemon juice

8 fl oz (250 ml) soured cream

1 × 6½ oz (185 g) tin lumpfish roe

3 drops of tabasco sauce

1 hard-boiled egg, chopped

chopped fresh parsley to garnish

Mix the gelatine and water in a cup. Stand the cup in a bowl of hot water and stir until the gelatine has dissolved. Mix together the mayonnaise and lemon juice, then add the soured cream. Add the gelatine mixture and beat the ingredients together well. Fold in the lumpfish roe with a knife and season with the tabasco sauce. Place in a dish and refrigerate for about 2 hours until set. Garnish with the chopped egg and parsley.

Lemon Hat Sardines

[SERVES 4]

I used to make this in France when I went to the Mediterranean with Lord and Lady Iliffe. We picked the lemons from the trees in their garden. They were large and smooth-skinned, delicious and juicy, not as sharp as those you sometimes get here. Meals were served on the patio, and Lady Iliffe bought me a basket to carry the food down the steps from the kitchen. You can use tuna instead of sardines for this recipe, but it has a coarser texture.

4 lemons

1 × 9 oz (250 g) tin sardines in oil, drained, skinned and boned

4 sprigs of watercress

4 slices wholemeal bread

1 oz (25 g) unsalted butter

Slice off a hat from the top of each lemon, and just enough from the bottom so that it will stand firmly on the plate. Using a teaspoon, scoop out the insides into a dish. Take out the membrane and pips and gently mash up the flesh with the sardines to a coarse mixture; you don't want a pulp. Return the filling to the lemons, place a sprig of watercress on top, and replace the hat at a jaunty angle. Cut the bread into small rounds with a pastry cutter, spread with the butter and arrange on individual plates with the stuffed lemons.

Rolled Seafood Pancakes

[SERVES 4]

This is a delicious starter or lunch dish which even freezes well made up, so is very easy. You can use left-over fish, or poach a fillet of cod or any other white fish in a little water or milk for about 5 minutes while you make the pancakes.

---

4 oz (100 g) plain flour

a pinch of salt

1 egg, beaten

½ pint (300 ml) milk

oil for frying

½ pint (300 ml) Béchamel Sauce (see page 194)

8 oz (225 g) white fish, cooked and flaked

2 oz (50 g) cooked shelled prawns

Pre-heat the oven to 375°F (190°C), gas mark 5. Place the flour and salt in a large bowl and pour the egg into a hollow in the centre. Gradually pour in the milk, beating until the batter is smooth and creamy. Heat a little oil in a frying pan and pour in enough batter just to cover the pan, tilting as you pour to spread the batter; this mixture will make 8 pancakes. Cook for about 1 minute until golden brown on the underside, then flip or turn the pancake and cook the other side. Continue cooking all the pancakes, stacking them flat once cooked.

Make the béchamel sauce and mix in the flaked fish and prawns. Pour a little sauce on to each pancake, roll it up, and place the pancakes in an ovenproof dish. Cover with greaseproof paper or foil to keep them moist, then place in the oven for about 20 minutes to heat through.

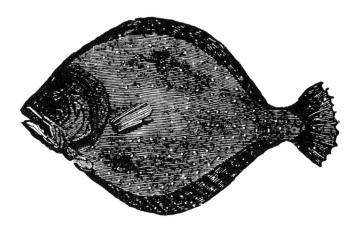

Gâteau Saumon

Illustrated on page 35

[SERVES 8]

This makes an unusual hot starter which can be mainly prepared in advance and left to cook. It was one of the most popular recipes collected by Lady Iliffe for her cookery booklets sold in aid of the Red Cross.

1½ lb (750 g) fresh salmon

salt

a few parsley stalks

1 teaspoon lemon juice

1 slice onion

1 small carrot

1 bay leaf

6 peppercorns

½ pint (300 ml) milk

8 oz (225 g) white bread, crusts removed

2 eggs

4 egg yolks

FOR THE SAUCE:

1 tablespoon oil

1 onion, finely chopped

1 clove garlic, finely chopped

8 oz (225 g) tomatoes, peeled and chopped

1 teaspoon mixed herbs

salt and freshly ground black pepper

Place the fish in a large saucepan, cover with lightly salted water and add the parsley stalks, lemon juice, slice of onion, carrot, bay leaf and peppercorns. Poach gently for about 15 minutes until the fish flakes when tested with a fork. Drain, remove the skin and bones and process the flesh until smooth.

Pre-heat the oven to 400°F (200°C), gas mark 6. Warm the milk in a large saucepan and soak the bread until softened. Add the fish, mix well and heat gently for a few minutes until thickened. Mix in the eggs and egg yolks. Place the mixture in an ovenproof dish and stand the dish in a roasting tin filled with water to come halfway up the sides of the dish. Bake for about 45 minutes until firm to the touch.

Meanwhile, make the sauce. Heat the oil and fry the onion and garlic gently until soft but not brown. Add the tomatoes and herbs and simmer gently for about 5 minutes until the sauce begins to thicken. Season to taste with salt and freshly ground black pepper. Pour it into a food processor and purée the sauce, then return it to the pan to re-heat. Turn the salmon gâteau on to a serving dish and serve the sauce separately.

Part Two

SOUPS

Chicken and Leek Soup

[SERVES 4]

Soups are a good way of using up left-overs. You can use them to start a meal, or make them extra thick and serve them with crusty bread or rolls and some salad to make a meal in themselves. You can always use a tin of chicken consommé as a base for soups, but this is obviously more expensive, and you get good results with stock or a stock cube. Having cut off the coarsest part of the leeks, I often use the soft green parts to make soup, then you can save the rest for a vegetable dish.

1 oz (25 g) unsalted butter

4 leeks, sliced

2 pints (1.2 litres) Chicken Stock (see page 198) or made with stock cubes

1 bouquet garni

salt and freshly ground black pepper

6 oz (175 g) cooked chicken, chopped

2 tablespoons natural yoghurt

1 tablespoon chopped fresh parsley

Melt the butter in a large saucepan and gently fry the leeks for about 5 minutes until transparent. Add the chicken stock and bouquet garni and season to taste with salt and freshly ground black pepper. Bring to the boil and simmer gently for about 10 minutes until the leeks are cooked. Pour the soup into a food processor and process until smooth, then return to the pan, add the chicken and heat. Pour into soup bowls and swirl in the yoghurt with a spoon to make a spiral in the centre. Sprinkle with chopped parsley to serve.

Croûtons make a nice garnish for any soups, but particularly the thick ones. Cut slices of bread into about $\frac{1}{4}$ in (5 mm) slices and remove the crusts. Then cut the slices into $\frac{1}{4}$ in (5 mm) cubes and fry them in a little unsalted butter until crisp and golden. You can either sprinkle them over the soup or serve them separately. For a change, you can add a little chopped garlic to the butter when you are frying. For parsley and cheese croûtons, toast the slices of bread on one side, then butter the other side and sprinkle with some grated cheese mixed with a little chopped fresh parsley and toast them before cutting them into squares.

Creamy Celeriac and Bacon Soup

[SERVES 4]

Celeriac is becoming more widely available now, and gives a stronger taste to soups than using celery. You can, of course, use celery instead, but try to buy white celery, which has more flavour, and be sure to use the leaves as well as the stems as these also add extra flavour.

1 oz (25 g) unsalted butter

2 onions, chopped

2 oz (50 g) bacon, chopped

1 medium potato, chopped

8 oz (225 g) celeriac, chopped

1 pint (600 ml) Chicken Stock (see page 198) or made with stock cubes

salt and freshly ground black pepper

¼ pint (150 ml) milk

1 egg yolk, beaten

Melt the butter in a large saucepan and gently fry the onions for about 5 minutes until transparent. Add the bacon, potato and celeriac and fry for a further 5 minutes. Add the stock and season to taste with salt and freshly ground black pepper. Bring to the boil, then simmer for about 30 minutes. Pour the soup into a food processor and process until smooth. Return to the pan, stir in the milk and re-heat gently for about 2 to 3 minutes without allowing the soup to boil. Stir in the egg yolk before serving.

Ham and Lentil Soup

[SERVES 4]

This makes a delicious thick soup for winter days. You can either use left-over ham or grill a few rashers of bacon to add flavour and texture to the finished soup.

6 oz (175 g) red lentils

1 oz (25 g) unsalted butter

1 onion, chopped

2 carrots, chopped

1 turnip, chopped

2 sticks celery, chopped

1 large tomato, skinned, deseeded and chopped

1 pint (600 ml) vegetable stock

salt and freshly ground black pepper

3 oz (75 g) cooked ham, chopped

Soak the lentils for 1 hour in cold water, then strain them. This softens the lentils and allows them to cook more easily.

Melt the butter in a large saucepan and fry the onion for about 3 minutes until transparent. Add the carrots, turnip, celery, lentils, tomato and stock, bring to the boil and simmer for about 30 minutes until all the vegetables are tender. Season to taste with salt and freshly ground black pepper. Pour the soup into a food processor and process until smooth. Return to the saucepan, add the ham and simmer over a low heat until heated through.

Tangy Carrot Soup

[SERVES 4]

Carrots are available all year round and make a hearty soup. The orange rind gives an extra tang to the flavour.

1 oz (25 g) unsalted butter

1 onion, sliced

1 lb (450 g) carrots, chopped

1 slice orange rind

2 pints (1.2 litres) Chicken Stock (see page 198) or made with stock cubes

salt and freshly ground black pepper

4 tablespoons natural yoghurt

2 tablespoons chopped fresh parsley

Melt the butter in a large saucepan and fry the onion for about 3 minutes until transparent. Add the carrots and cook gently for a further 5 minutes. Add the orange rind and stock, season with salt and freshly ground black pepper, bring to the boil and simmer gently for about 20 minutes. Pour into a food processor and process until smooth. Then return to the saucepan, add the yoghurt and re-heat but do not allow the soup to boil. Pour into a serving dish and sprinkle with chopped fresh parsley.

Stilton and Celery Soup

[SERVES 4]

I love the strong taste of Stilton, and this is a good recipe for using up any odd pieces of cheese which are left over. You can adjust the amount of cheese you use to suit your own taste.

It is so simple to process soups now, and you can easily vary the texture. Some of you may have seen us pushing soups through a tammy cloth on *The Victorian Kitchen* television series, which was really arm-aching work.

1 oz (25 g) unsalted butter

1 onion, finely chopped

1 head celery, chopped

1 medium-sized potato, chopped

2 pints (1.2 litres) Chicken Stock (see page 198) or made with stock cubes

salt and freshly ground black pepper

4 oz (100 g) Stilton cheese, crumbled or grated

Melt the butter in a large saucepan and gently fry the onion for about 3 minutes until transparent. Add the celery and potato and fry for a further 5 minutes. Add the stock and season to taste with salt and freshly ground black pepper. Bring to the boil and simmer gently for about 30 minutes. Pour into a food processor and process until smooth. Return the soup to the pan, bring it to the boil, then remove from the heat and stir in the Stilton before serving.

Vegetable Soup with Cheesy Dumplings

Illustrated on page 36

[SERVES 4]

This is a wonderful soup for using whatever vegetables you have to hand. You can add a few lentils for variety, or throw in some chopped cooked chicken, ham or lamb, or add a handful of soup pasta for the last few minutes of cooking.

1 oz (25 g) unsalted butter
1 onion, sliced
1 lb (450 g) mixed vegetables (carrots, turnip, swede, celery, cauliflower, parsnip, potato), sliced or chopped
2 pints (1.2 litres) vegetable stock
1 oz (25 g) pearl barley
1 bouquet garni
salt and freshly ground black pepper

FOR THE CHEESY DUMPLINGS:

3 oz (75 g) self-raising flour
1 oz (25 g) shredded suet
1½ oz (40 g) Cheddar cheese, grated
2 tablespoons milk

Melt the butter in a large saucepan and fry the onion gently for about 3 minutes until transparent. Add the vegetables, stock, pearl barley and bouquet garni, bring to the boil and simmer for about 30 minutes. Season to taste with salt and freshly ground black pepper.

While the soup is cooking, make the dumplings. Mix the flour, suet and cheese and bind with just enough milk to make a soft scone-like dough. Shape into about 16 dumplings and drop into the boiling soup for the last 20 minutes of cooking time.

Velvety Potato Soup

[SERVES 4]

The cream in this recipe gives a nice velvety finish to the soup. Serve it with chunks of crusty wholemeal bread.

---

1 oz (25 g) unsalted butter

---

2 onions, sliced

---

1 lb (450 g) potatoes, chopped

---

2 pints (1.2 litres) Chicken Stock (see page 198) or made with stock cubes

---

1 bouquet garni

---

salt and freshly ground black pepper

---

4 tablespoons single cream

---

chopped fresh chives to garnish

Melt the butter in a large saucepan and sweat the onions for about 5 minutes until transparent. Add the chopped potatoes and fry for a further 5 minutes but do not allow to brown. Add the stock and bouquet garni, season with salt and freshly ground black pepper, bring to the boil and simmer gently for about 20 minutes. Remove the bouquet garni, pour into a food processor and process until smooth. Return to the saucepan, stir in the cream and re-heat but do not allow to boil. Pour into a serving dish and sprinkle with chopped fresh chives.

Summer Watercress Soup

[SERVES 4]

Use the whole bunch of watercress for this soup, stalks and all, as there is more flavour in the stalks than the leaves. It is best to make the soup as late as possible before serving, otherwise it will lose its lovely green colour. If that does happen, dip a skewer in a pot of green food colour and gently stir it into the finished soup. Serve it with crispy croûtons (see page 26).

1 tablespoon oil

2 oz (50 g) unsalted butter

1 small onion, chopped

1 large potato, chopped

2 bunches watercress, chopped

2 pints (1.2 litres) Chicken Stock (see page 198) or made with stock cubes

salt and freshly ground black pepper

grated nutmeg to garnish

Heat the oil and half the butter in a large saucepan and fry the onion for about 3 minutes until transparent. Add the potato and fry for a further 5 minutes. Add the chopped watercress and stock and season to taste with salt and freshly ground black pepper. Bring to the boil and simmer gently for about 20 minutes. Pour into a food processor and process until smooth, then strain back into the saucepan, stir in the remaining butter and re-heat. Pour into a serving dish and sprinkle with nutmeg.

Cream of Spinach Soup

[SERVES 4]

Some people find onions upset their stomach and do not use them, but they do give something special to so many dishes, especially soups. This soup should be prepared as late as possible so that it keeps its lovely green colour.

2 oz (50 g) unsalted butter

1 onion, finely chopped

1 lb (450 g) cooked spinach, chopped

1 oz (25 g) plain flour

½ pint (300 ml) Chicken Stock (see page 198) or made with stock cubes

1 pint (600 ml) milk

salt and freshly ground black pepper

a pinch of nutmeg

4 tablespoons single cream

Melt the butter in a large saucepan and fry the onion over a low heat for about 3 minutes until transparent. Add the spinach and cook for a further 5 minutes. Remove from the heat and stir in the flour. Add the stock, return to the heat and bring to the boil, stirring until the soup begins to thicken. Stir in the milk, season to taste with salt, freshly ground black pepper and a pinch of nutmeg and simmer gently for about 20 minutes. Pour the soup into a food processor and process until smooth. Return to the pan to re-heat. Pour into a serving dish and stir in the cream.

Minty Pea Soup

[SERVES 4]

Adding some chopped mint to this pea soup gives it a delicious minty taste which makes it quite unusual, even though it is so easy to prepare. You can vary the recipe and make it into more of a light meal by adding some chopped ham or pieces of grilled bacon. As it is, it is lovely served with crispy croûtons (see page 26).

1 tablespoon oil

1 oz (25 g) unsalted butter

1 onion, chopped

1 medium potato, chopped

10 oz (275 g) frozen garden peas

1½ pints (900 ml) Chicken Stock (see page 198) or made with stock cubes

2 tablespoons chopped mint leaves

salt and freshly ground black pepper

¼ pint (150 ml) single cream

Heat the oil and butter in a large saucepan and fry the onion and potato gently for about 5 minutes. Add the peas, stock and most of the chopped mint, season to taste with salt and freshly ground black pepper, bring to the boil and simmer for about 15 minutes. Pour the soup into a food processor and process until smooth, then rub the purée through a sieve or mouli to remove any remaining pea husks. Return the soup to the pan, stir in all but 2 tablespoons of the cream and re-heat the soup without boiling. Pour into a serving dish, swirl in the remaining cream and sprinkle with a little chopped mint.

For a delicious and quick French Onion Soup, add some sliced browned onions to a good proprietary brand of beef consommé. Grate some cheese on to pieces of French bread and brown them under the grill before floating them on the soup in the bowls.

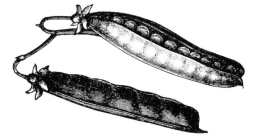

Discussing which vegetables to use with Harry Dodson, my Victorian Kitchen *helpmate.*

OVERLEAF] *Oeufs Basildon (page 18); Gâteau Saumon (page 23).*

Vegetable Soup with Cheesy Dumplings (page 29).

OPPOSITE] *Salmon Coulibiac (page 56).*

OVERLEAF] *Parsley Trout with Green Noodles (page 54); Smoked Haddock Terrine (page 50).*

Spring Fruit Soup

[SERVES 4]

This was one of the recipes we made in *The Victorian Kitchen* television series. I thought it would be awful, but it really worked out well! It has a slightly sharp flavour from the rhubarb which is most unusual in a soup. It might be a bit of an acquired taste, but it is certainly worth trying. I generally use a tinned consommé which works well. Some people have told me they found the soup a little too sharp, as rhubarb sticks can be large, small, young or old. Try it with about two sticks at first; then you may like to add a little more.

---

2 sticks rhubarb, chopped

2 oz (50 g) unsalted butter

1 onion, sliced

1 carrot, sliced

1 oz (25 g) cooked ham or bacon, chopped

1½ pints (900 ml) beef consommé

1 oz (25 g) breadcrumbs

salt

a pinch of cayenne pepper

Blanch the rhubarb in boiling water for 3 or 4 minutes, then drain. Melt the butter in a large saucepan, add the onion and fry gently for about 3 minutes until transparent. Add the rhubarb, carrot and ham or bacon and cook over a low heat for about 10 minutes until tender. Add the consommé and breadcrumbs, bring to the boil and simmer for about 15 minutes. Skim off any fat which has come to the surface by drawing a piece of kitchen paper across the top. Season to taste with salt and cayenne pepper. Pour the soup into a food processor and process until smooth. Return to the pan to re-heat and serve with croûtons (see page 26).

OPPOSITE] *Crispy-Topped Scallops (page 59).*

Borscht

[SERVES 4]

This famous chilled soup is very easy and makes a nice appetiser, especially if it is served with a spoonful of yoghurt and crispy croûtons (see page 26). You can, of course, make your own consommé, but using a good proprietary brand will save a lot of time and effort. Make sure you buy ordinary cooked beetroot which has not been put in vinegar. The soup is also delicious served hot with a spoonful of yoghurt or cream in the bowls.

---

2 lb (1 kg) cooked beetroot or raw beetroot, peeled and grated

---

1 onion, chopped

---

2 pints (1.2 litres) beef consommé

---

2 tablespoons lemon juice

---

4 tablespoons dry sherry

---

salt and freshly ground black pepper

---

4 tablespoons natural yoghurt or soured cream

---

2 tablespoons chopped fresh chives

If you are using uncooked beetroot, add the beetroot and onion to the consommé in a large saucepan, bring to the boil and simmer, covered, for about 40 minutes. If you are using cooked beetroot, simply bring the consommé to the boil and add the beetroot and onion. Remove the saucepan from the heat and leave it to stand for 2 hours. Strain the liquid and discard the vegetables. Add the lemon juice and sherry to the liquid, season to taste with salt and freshly ground black pepper and refrigerate until well chilled. Serve with a whirl of yoghurt or soured cream and sprinkle with chopped chives.

Vichyssoise

[SERVES 4]

Ideal for summer dinner parties, Vichyssoise can be prepared and cooked in advance. It really does need a proper chicken stock to taste its best, as stock cubes can be too salt for the delicate flavour. If you do use a stock cube, don't make the stock too strong, and add less salt when seasoning.

1 oz (25 g) unsalted butter

1 onion, finely chopped

1 medium potato, chopped

12 oz (350 g) leeks, sliced

2 pints (1.2 litres) Chicken Stock (see page 198)

salt and freshly ground black pepper

4 tablespoons single cream

chopped fresh chives to garnish

Melt the butter in a large saucepan and gently fry the onion and potato for about 3 minutes until the onion is transparent. Add the leeks and stock and season to taste with salt and freshly ground black pepper. Bring to the boil and simmer gently for about 30 minutes until the vegetables are tender. Pour into a food processor and process until smooth. Stir in the cream. Pour into a serving bowl and chill. Sprinkle with the chopped chives before serving.

I received lots of letters from people who watched the television series The Victorian Kitchen. *Many were people in their 80s who wanted to talk about the times they spent in service, and said how much watching the series brought back to them.*

One elderly lady asked if I had ever folded my hanky into a little rabbit and whether I could remember how it was done – I certainly did! We sometimes used to make these little rabbits at morning prayers, and when you pulled them, the tail wagged. We used to get dreadful fits of the giggles!

At this one particular house, we had prayers before breakfast each morning, which was quite unusual in those days. The lady of the house was very religious, and always read the Bible every day. She lived her religion, and did an awful lot of good in the village. She helped everyone she could and always brought out the potential in people. My mother read her Bible regularly, and she loved to read The Pilgrim's Progress; *she would always go back to that if she had no library books.*

Part Three

FISH

Seafood and Basil Casserole

[SERVES 4]

You can include whatever fish you like in this recipe, almost like a paella. I like it with a few prawns, some white and some smoked fish. I could be a campaigner for smoked fish! It just seems to have something which lifts recipes out of the plain and dull.

If you do not have fresh basil for this recipe, use pesto sauce, just a small piece on the end of a teaspoon – you can always add more to suit your taste, but it is much stronger than fresh basil. Keep it in the fridge. It tends to lose colour when opened, but do not be put off by this.

2 fl oz (50 ml) olive oil

4 medium-sized onions, sliced

2 cloves garlic, crushed

1 red pepper, deseeded and sliced

1 green pepper, deseeded and sliced

1 tablespoon chopped fresh basil

1 tablespoon chopped fresh parsley

1 lb (450 g) tomatoes, blanched, peeled and chopped

$\frac{1}{4}$ teaspoon chilli powder

2 lb (1 kg) mixed fish fillets, cut into bite-sized pieces

$\frac{1}{4}$ teaspoon salt

$\frac{1}{4}$ teaspoon freshly ground black pepper

1 tablespoon white wine vinegar

Pre-heat the oven to 300°F (150°C), gas mark 2. Heat the oil over a moderate heat in a flameproof casserole, then add the onions and garlic. Fry gently for about 5 minutes until the onions are translucent, then add the peppers, basil, parsley, tomatoes and chilli powder. Cover the casserole and put it into the oven for about 1 to 1$\frac{1}{2}$ hours until the mixture resembles a thick sauce. Stir in the fish and season with salt and freshly ground black pepper. Return to the oven for about 20 to 30 minutes until the fish is cooked, then stir in the vinegar.

This casserole is delicious served hot with a green vegetable and boiled or mashed potatoes, or it can be served cold with new potatoes and a green salad.

I was born in Yattendon and now live in my parents' home. But there are very few in the village now who grew up here. I have been collecting some old photographs of the area to give to my daughter and I was going to mount them all in an album when I retired, but there never seems to be the time! There used to be an old elm tree in the middle of the village. It was hollow, and there was a hole like a little door in it so you could go into the middle. We kept the tree until the Dutch elm disease but then it died.

Cod with Caper Sauce

[SERVES 4]

I think the flavour of a caper sauce complements cod nicely, and this is a simple dish to prepare for a family meal.

4 cod cutlets

½ pint (300 ml) Fish Stock (see page 199)

¼ pint (150 ml) dry white wine

salt and cayenne pepper

1 tablespoon cornflour dissolved in 2 tablespoons water

¼ pint (150 ml) double cream

2 tablespoons capers

1 tablespoon chopped fresh parsley or dill

Place the cod, fish stock and wine in a saucepan and season with salt and cayenne pepper. Bring to the boil, cover and poach gently for about 10 minutes until just cooked. Remove the cutlets to a serving dish and keep them warm. Return the pan to the heat and bring to a brisk boil. Remove from the heat and add the dissolved cornflour (or you may find it easier to add the juices to the cornflour). Bring back to the boil and simmer for about 3 minutes, stirring continuously, to cook the cornflour, otherwise it may taste raw. Reduce the heat, stir in the cream and capers and cook for a further 2 minutes but do not allow the sauce to boil. Pour over the fish and serve sprinkled with fresh parsley or dill to give a little colour.

Chicken Turbot Hollandaise

[SERVES 4]

Chicken turbot is a small fish not often found today, but if you are lucky enough to find one, it makes a nice dinner party dish, although you can use small but nice thick fillets of turbot instead. Unless you have someone to do this for you, you'll have to take your drink to the kitchen and stay with it as it doesn't like waiting!

1 chicken turbot or 4 turbot fillets

salt and freshly ground black pepper

2 oz (50 g) unsalted butter, cut into pieces

½ pint (300 ml) Hollandaise Sauce (see page 194)

Pre-heat the oven to 350°F (180°C), gas mark 4. Place the fish in a well buttered gratin dish, season with salt and freshly ground black pepper, and dot with the butter. Seal with buttered greaseproof paper or foil and bake in the oven for about 20 minutes until soft. Meanwhile, make the hollandaise sauce and have the grill nice and hot. Take the fish out of the oven, remove the foil and pour over the hollandaise sauce. Place under the grill until lightly browned and serve immediately.

Haddock Soufflé

[SERVES 4]

Don't be put off by the word 'soufflé'; try this dish on the family before you embark on it for guests. It is best cooked in a shallow soufflé dish as it won't rise up like an ordinary soufflé. It will only rise up a couple of inches and should be moist in the middle and browned on top. You must cook it in a *bain marie* – a tray of water – as the steam keeps it moist; otherwise it will go hard round the sides. Haddock or whiting are the best fish to use, and it is also nice with a Hollandaise Sauce (see page 194). It is quite a filling dish, so you don't really need anything else with it.

---

1 oz (25 g) fresh white breadcrumbs

2½ fl oz (65 ml) milk, boiling

---

8 oz (225 g) cooked haddock fillets

---

1 tablespoon lemon juice

½ pint (300 ml) Béchamel Sauce (see page 194)

---

salt

---

a pinch of paprika

---

1 tablespoon chopped fresh parsley

---

3 egg yolks, beaten

---

4 egg whites, stiffly beaten

Pre-heat the oven to 350°F (180°C), gas mark 4. Place the breadcrumbs in a bowl and pour over the boiling milk. Leave to soak. Flake the fish into a food processor with the lemon juice and process until smooth. Make the béchamel sauce, but leave out about 2 tablespoons of milk. Stir the fish purée and the soaked breadcrumbs into the sauce, season to taste with salt and paprika and stir in the parsley. Beat in the egg yolks, then gently fold in the stiffly beaten whites. Turn into a shallow well buttered dish, and stand the dish in a tray of water. Bake for about 30 minutes until cooked through and nicely browned on top.

Everyone has a favourite cookery book and my cookery 'bible' is Connie Spry. Although I have loads of cookery books, that is the most thumbed book in my collection. I can understand it because I have lived with that type of cooking all my life and that was my grounding. I also have two Sheila Hutchings books of regional country recipes which I like. I used her Christmas pudding recipe when she first started writing years ago and I have never changed it. The other cookery writer I like is Robert Carrier. They all produce recipes you can prepare without a staff and lots of equipment!

I read lots of food magazines all the time, like Good Food *magazine and* Taste. *It keeps you up to date with all the new ideas and what is going on.*

Smoky Fish Cakes

[SERVES 4]

I love fish cakes, particularly made with smoked and white fish, but you can use any fish you like, or make them with salmon for a change, tinned or fresh. Wholemeal breadcrumbs are nice if you are a health fan, but I prefer white.

8 oz (225 g) smoked haddock
8 oz (225 g) white fish
3 oz (75 g) unsalted butter
1 lb (450 g) potatoes
salt and freshly ground black pepper
1 tablespoon chopped fresh parsley or dill
1 egg yolk
flour for dredging
1 egg, beaten
4 oz (100 g) fresh white breadcrumbs
oil for frying

Pre-heat the oven to 350°F (180°C), gas mark 4. Line a tin with foil, place the fish in the tin with about 1 oz (25 g) butter to keep it moist, cover with foil and bake for about 15 minutes until just cooked. Meanwhile, cook the potatoes in boiling water, then drain and mash them dry. Season to taste with salt and freshly ground black pepper and mix in the chopped parsley or dill and the egg yolk. Flake the fish, add it to the potatoes and mix together gently.

Put the mixture on to a plate and flatten it to about $\frac{1}{2}$ in (1 cm) thick, then leave it to cool. Turn it on to a floured board and either cut cakes with a 2 in (5 cm) cutter, or mould with your hands into cakes the size you require. Dredge with flour, then coat with beaten egg and roll in breadcrumbs. Shallow fry in a little oil for about 5 minutes on each side until cooked through and golden brown.

Smoked Haddock Terrine

Illustrated on page 39

[SERVES 4]

Anice dish for the family, Smoked Haddock Terrine is also special enough for a party. You can garnish it with the olives and cucumber, or use sliced tomatoes with sprigs of watercress. For a change, a layer of cooked puréed spinach is nice in the middle to give the terrine a little green stripe.

$1\frac{1}{2}$ lb (750 g) smoked haddock

4 oz (100 g) fromage frais

4 fl oz (120 ml) oil

4 eggs

juice of 1 lemon

4 oz (100 g) smoked salmon, cut into small pieces

6 lettuce leaves

4 stuffed olives, sliced

1 in (2.5 cm) piece of cucumber, finely sliced

a few sprigs of fresh dill

Pre-heat the oven to 350°F (180°C), gas mark 4. Place the haddock, fromage frais, oil, eggs and lemon juice in a food processor and process until smooth. Place half the mixture in a greased 2 lb (1 kg) loaf tin. Place snips of smoked salmon down the middle and cover with the remaining mixture. Cover with greased foil and place in a baking tray filled with water to come halfway up the sides of the loaf tin. Place in the hot oven for 5 minutes, then turn down the oven to 300°F (150°C), gas mark 2 and bake for a further 40 minutes.

Leave to cool in the tin, and turn out on to the lettuce leaves on a serving plate when the terrine is barely warm. Place a line of olive slices down the centre, and slices of cucumber down each side, then add a few sprigs of dill.

Golden Crispy Fish Pie

[SERVES 4]

Mixing cheese and breadcrumbs on top of the dish makes a nice crunchy top, better than cheese alone, which can sometimes go stringy.

---

8 oz (225 g) white fish

---

8 oz (225 g) smoked haddock

---

1 small onion, chopped

½ pint (300 ml) Béchamel Sauce (see page 194) made with the fish liquor made up to quantity with milk

---

2 oz (50 g) mushrooms, sliced

---

1 hard-boiled egg, chopped

---

1 tablespoon fresh chopped parsley

---

3 oz (75 g) Cheddar cheese, grated

---

3 oz (75 g) fresh white breadcrumbs

Pre-heat the oven to 375°F (190°C), gas mark 5. Place the fish and onion in a saucepan with a little water, bring to the boil and poach gently for about 10 minutes until cooked. Drain and save the liquor to make the béchamel sauce. Flake the fish and fold it lightly into the cooked sauce with the mushrooms, hard-boiled egg and parsley. Place the mixture in a pie dish. Mix together the grated cheese and breadcrumbs, sprinkle them over the top and bake for 15 to 20 minutes until the fish is heated through and the top is crispy and golden.

Creamy Kedgeree

[SERVES 4]

Rice forms the base of this dish, with fish, hard-boiled eggs, parsley, butter and, for me, cream! Once again, I like to use cooked smoked haddock – Finnan if you can find a nice big one – or some fresh cooked salmon if you've any left over from a party. A few bits of smoked salmon also give it a kick. You can vary the amount of fish, but I prefer plenty of fish to rice.

---

6 oz (175 g) rice

---

3 hard-boiled eggs

8–10 oz (225–275 g) cooked flaked fish, or to taste

---

salt and freshly ground black pepper

---

3 oz (75 g) unsalted butter, cut into small pieces

¼ pint (150 ml) single or double cream

---

1 tablespoon chopped fresh parsley

Pre-heat the oven to 350°F (180°C), gas mark 4. Cook the rice in boiling salted water until just tender, then drain. Shell the eggs, then chop each one into about 8 pieces and carefully fold into the rice with the flaked fish. Do this gently so you keep nice big flakes of fish and the mixture does not become a mush. Season to taste with salt and freshly ground black pepper, and stir in the butter and cream. Place in an ovenproof dish and heat through in the oven for about 15 minutes. This avoids too much stirring which breaks up the fish. When hot, serve sprinkled with parsley.

Dover Sole Colbert

[SERVES 4]

For me this is the king of the sea, far surpassing any other fish; it is absolutely super and well worth the trouble. You can serve it with new potatoes and French beans, but I like it just on its own.

---

4 Dover sole, skinned, deheaded and trimmed

---

2 tablespoons plain flour, seasoned with salt and freshly ground black pepper

---

3 oz (75 g) unsalted butter

---

1 tablespoon finely chopped fresh parsley

---

1 tablespoon lemon juice

Slit the fish down the middle from top to tail on one side, and roll them in the seasoned flour. Melt about 1 oz (25 g) of the butter and brush the fish all over with melted butter. Place them on foil, slit side down, and grill for about 4 to 5 minutes. Turn them over and grill the other side. Meanwhile, melt the remaining butter in a saucepan and add the finely chopped parsley and lemon juice. Lift the sole on to a serving plate, slide a knife under the slit, turn back and remove the bone. Fold the fish back again. Pour over the parsley butter and serve immediately.

Goujons of Sole with Fried Parsley

[SERVES 4]

Sole is my favourite fish for this recipe, but you can use plaice. The fried parsley makes the dish that little bit different. Lady Iliffe always used to say, 'You won't forget the parsley, will you, Mrs Mott?' I usually get the parsley ready in the morning and wrap it in a cloth so that it's really dry, as it can spit when you dunk it in the hot fat.

---

4 fillets of sole

---

2 tablespoons plain flour, seasoned with salt and freshly ground black pepper

---

1 egg, beaten

---

4 oz (100 g) fresh white breadcrumbs

---

oil for deep frying

---

a good bunch of parsley, washed, thoroughly dried and cut into snippets

---

$\frac{1}{2}$ pint (300 ml) Hollandaise Sauce (see page 194) or Tartare Sauce (see page 195)

Cut the fillets into strips about the size of your little finger. Roll them in the seasoned flour, then dip in the egg and roll in breadcrumbs. Heat the frying oil and fry the fish in hot deep fat for about 5 minutes until cooked and browned. Drain the fish, place on a serving dish and keep it warm. Place the parsley in a frying basket. Carefully – it can spit – dunk the parsley into the hot fat for a few seconds to crisp it, then drain it and scatter it over the fish. Serve with the hollandaise or tartare sauce.

Herrings with Mustard Sauce

[SERVES 4]

I make this sauce with Dijon or Meaux mustard as they have a piquant flavour.

4 herrings, filleted, washed and dried

1 tablespoon lemon juice

2 eggs, well beaten

1 teaspoon Dijon mustard

salt and freshly ground black pepper

2 oz (50 g) plain flour

2 oz (50 g) unsalted butter

FOR THE SAUCE:

4 oz (100 g) unsalted butter

1 teaspoon made mustard

Sprinkle the herring fillets with the lemon juice and place on one side. In a shallow plate (I use a soup plate), mix the eggs, mustard, salt and freshly ground black pepper and beat until well blended. Sprinkle the flour on to a large plate. Dip the fillets into the egg mixture then roll in the flour, coating well all over. Melt the butter in a large frying pan and heat until foaming. Add the fillets and cook for about 3 minutes on each side. Place the fish on a serving dish and keep them warm.

To make the sauce, melt the butter with the mustard and season to taste. Heat through, then pour over the fish.

Rollmop Herrings

[SERVES 4]

R ollmop herrings make a delicious lunch or a nice starter. They are easy to make and keep for about a fortnight in the fridge. You don't actually cook the fish, but the marinade has the effect of cooking the fish for you. It is important that you use malt vinegar.

2 oz (50 g) cooking salt

½ pint (300 ml) water

8 fresh herring fillets

½ pint (300 ml) malt vinegar

8 small onions, peeled

1 teaspoon pickling spice

Mix the salt and water and soak the fillets for at least 2 hours. Lift the fish out of the water, rinse, drain, and put in a dish. Cover with the vinegar and leave overnight. Remove the fish from the vinegar and drain. Lay skin side down on a plate and place a small onion just above the tail. Roll up the fish, secure with a cocktail stick and pack into a glass jar. I nip the stick off close to the fish as it allows you to pack them tighter into the jar. Bring the vinegar and pickling spice to the boil and simmer for 15 minutes. Leave it to get cold, then strain it over the herrings. Seal and allow to mature for a few days.

Parsley Trout with Green Noodles

Illustrated on page 38

[SERVES 4]

This dish is easier if you talk to your fishmonger and get him to fillet the trout for you. Once that is done, it is quite simple and delicious.

4 trout, filleted
¼ pint (150 ml) dry white wine
¼ pint (150 ml) water
1 bouquet garni
8 oz (225 g) dried green noodles
4 tablespoons fromage frais
salt and freshly ground black pepper
1 tablespoon chopped fresh parsley
4 lemon wedges to garnish

Place the filleted fish in a large saucepan and barely cover with a mixture of half wine and half water. Don't drown the poor chaps! Add the bouquet garni, cover and cook gently for about 15 minutes until cooked through. Cook the green noodles to taste in boiling salted water. Drain them and put them into a serving dish. Place the fillets of trout on top. Carefully warm the fromage frais, but do not allow it to get too hot, season to taste with salt and freshly ground black pepper, add the chopped parsley and spoon the sauce over the fillets. Serve with lemon wedges.

Smoked Trout Pâté

[SERVES 4]

You can serve this pâté as a starter, or it makes a nice light lunch dish served with a mixed salad.

2 lb (1 kg) smoked trout, skinned, boned and flaked
4 oz (100 g) fromage frais
4 oz (100 g) cream cheese
1 tablespoon horseradish sauce
2 tablespoons lemon juice
freshly ground black pepper
1 tablespoon chopped fresh parsley
½ lemon, sliced
sprigs of parsley to garnish

Place the fish and fromage frais in a food processor and process until smooth. Add the remaining ingredients and process again until it is blended and as smooth as you fancy. Place in ramekin dishes, smooth the tops and garnish with a little round of lemon and a sprig of parsley for colour. Serve with melba toast or rolled brown bread and butter.

Cold Summer Trout

[SERVES 4]

This dish is nice with parsley, or any other herbs you like with fish. It makes a lovely summer meal, served with a few salads.

---

1 tablespoon olive oil

---

4 trout

---

1 onion, thinly sliced

---

1 large tomato, peeled and sliced

---

1 tablespoon chopped fresh parsley

---

grated rind of 1 lemon

---

2 bay leaves

---

12 black peppercorns

---

1 clove garlic, crushed

---

salt

¼ pint (150 ml) white wine or cider

¼ pint (150 ml) wine vinegar

---

sprigs of parsley to garnish

Pre-heat the oven to 300°F (150°C), gas mark 2. Heat the olive oil in a frying pan and fry the trout lightly for about 4 minutes. Drain the fish and keep the oil on one side. Grease an ovenproof dish. Place half the onion, tomato, parsley, lemon rind, bay leaves and peppercorns in layers in the dish. Lay the trout on this mixture and cover it with the same layers in reverse, finishing with the onion. Heat the oil and add the crushed garlic with some salt and the wine or cider and wine vinegar. Bring to the boil, then pour over the trout. Cover with foil and bake for about 15 minutes or until cooked. (The time will vary depending on the size of the fish.) Leave overnight to cool.

Next day, remove the heads and skin of the trout (if you can, this is not vital), and place the fish on a clean dish. Pour the remaining mixture into a food processor and process until smooth. Pour the mixture over the trout and garnish with parsley sprigs.

Salmon Coulibiac

Illustrated on page 37

[SERVES 4]

You can use left-overs of salmon to make this dish, or fresh fillets. There is an easy recipe for puff pastry at the end of the book, but frozen puff pastry is just as good, providing you thaw it to the maker's instructions. You don't have to serve a sauce, but I like to serve it with a little hollandaise, as the filling can be a bit dry.

---

1 lb (450 g) salmon fillet

---

4 oz (100 g) unsalted butter

---

1 small onion, chopped

---

4 oz (100 g) long-grain rice

---

salt and freshly ground black pepper

---

1 pint (600 ml) water

---

4 oz (100 g) mushrooms, sliced

---

2 hard-boiled eggs, chopped

1½ tablespoons chopped fresh parsley

---

*2 teaspoons chopped fresh dill
or a pinch of dried dill*

---

8 oz (225 g) Puff Pastry (see page 201)

---

1 egg, beaten

½ pint (300 ml) Hollandaise Sauce (see page 194)

Pre-heat the oven to 325°F (160°C), gas mark 3. Place the salmon in buttered foil in a baking dish and bake for about 30 minutes until cooked. Allow to cool, then skin the fillets and flake. Melt 3 oz (75 g) of the butter in a frying pan and fry the onion for about 3 minutes until soft. Add the rice and a good pinch of salt and freshly ground black pepper. Stir and turn until the rice is coated with butter. Add the water, bring to the boil and cook until the liquid is absorbed, adding a little more water if the rice is not cooked. Meanwhile, melt the remaining butter in a small saucepan and soften the mushrooms, but do not overcook them. Add the mushrooms, salmon and eggs to the rice mixture with the parsley and dill. Allow to cool.

Roll out the pastry into a rectangle about 12 × 22 in (30 × 55 cm). Place on a greased baking sheet, lay the filling down the centre, brush the edges with beaten egg and bring the ends up to form a roll, making sure it is sealed tight. I usually turn mine over to get the join underneath. Make any little bits of pastry left over into leaves and stick them on to the top with beaten egg. Brush the roll with beaten egg, make one or two holes with the point of a knife to let the steam escape and bake in a pre-heated oven at 400°F (200°C), gas mark 6, for about 40 minutes until nice and brown. Serve with the hollandaise sauce.

Salmon Dill in Filo Pastry

[SERVES 4]

Filo pastry is being used more nowadays and is available frozen in most supermarkets, although this recipe can be made with puff pastry – either home-made or frozen – if you prefer. I have tried a little experiment with filo. Let the filo thaw out, unroll it to full length and cut it in half across. Put a piece of freezer layering paper on a baking sheet and place a piece of filo on top, then continue to layer paper and filo until the pastry is used up. Put it in the freezer to firm up again, then take it out so that you can remove the baking tray and pack the filo between two sheets of cardboard. This way you can remove as many sheets as you require. Filo is very good-tempered and will refreeze several times, but can't stand being banged around.

---

4 sheets filo pastry

---

2 oz (50 g) unsalted butter

---

1 lb (450 g) salmon fillet, cut into 4 portions

---

salt and freshly ground black pepper

---

1 tablespoon chopped fresh dill

---

1 egg, beaten

Pre-heat the oven to 400°F (200°C), gas mark 6. Place the sheets of pastry on a board. Melt half the butter and brush the first pastry sheet well with the melted butter. Lay the second sheet on top, brush with melted butter and continue with the remaining sheets. Cut the pastry into 4. Season the salmon portions with salt, freshly ground black pepper and dill, and place one on each piece of pastry. Cut the remaining butter into 4 and put a knob of butter on each portion. Brush the edges of the pastry with beaten egg, then seal into 4 parcels. Turn them over and place them on a baking sheet so the join is underneath, then glaze the pastry with the remaining egg. Bake for about 10 minutes, then turn down the oven to about 350°F (180°C), gas mark 4, for a further 10 minutes until the salmon is cooked and the pastry browned. Serve the parcels on their own, or make a Hollandaise Sauce (see page 194) or Tartare Sauce (see page 195).

Creamy Prawn Curry

[SERVES 3 TO 4]

A curry makes a nice easy meal, and you can vary the strength of the curry, and the ingredients, to suit your taste. Prawns curry well, as do pork left-overs.

4 tablespoons oil

1 onion, chopped

2 teaspoons curry powder, or to taste

1 tablespoon plain flour

4 ripe tomatoes, skinned, deseeded and chopped

1 small clove garlic, chopped

1 tablespoon wine vinegar

1 lb (450 g) peeled prawns

1 egg

½ pint (150 ml) single cream or fromage frais

Heat the oil in a frying pan and fry the onion for about 3 minutes until soft but not brown. Add the curry powder and fry for a further few minutes. Add the flour, tomatoes, garlic and wine vinegar and cook for about 5 minutes. Add the prawns and heat through. Beat the egg with the cream or fromage frais and fold this into the prawn curry. Re-heat but do not allow the curry to boil. Serve with boiled rice.

Lobster Mousse

[SERVES 4]

This is a delicious mousse which makes a nice starter for a dinner party. You can fold in a couple of whipped egg whites if you wish to keep the mousse light. Remember to whip them only until they are fluffy, otherwise they can be quite heavy.

12 oz (350 g) lobster meat, fresh or tinned, finely chopped

3 tablespoons Creamy Mayonnaise (see page 197)

1 × ½ oz (15 g) sachet gelatine powder

½ pint (300 ml) double or whipping cream, lightly whipped

salt and freshly ground black pepper

2 dashes of Worcestershire sauce

1 × 1 oz (30 g) sachet aspic powder

1 × 1 in (2.5 cm) piece of cucumber, thinly sliced

Mix the chopped lobster meat with the mayonnaise. Dissolve the gelatine in 3 tablespoons of water over a pan of hot water, then allow to cool. Add to the lobster mixture. When it is beginning to set, fold in the whipped cream, season to taste with salt and freshly ground black pepper, and add the Worcestershire sauce. Turn into a soufflé dish until set. Make up the aspic jelly according to the instructions and garnish the top of the mousse with a thin layer of aspic. Lay some slices of cucumber around the edge, then cover with another thin layer of aspic.

Crispy-Topped Scallops

Illustrated on page 40

[SERVES 4]

Scallops can be simply grilled or served on buttered toast. Or, as a change, you can make Curry Sauce (see page 193) instead of the white sauce, and mix some grated cheese with the breadcrumbs.

---

12 scallops, washed and trimmed

¼ pint (150 ml) dry white wine

¼ pint (150 ml) water

---

1 small onion, chopped

---

1 bouquet garni

---

salt and freshly ground black pepper

---

3 oz (75 g) unsalted butter

---

4 oz (100 g) mushrooms, sliced

---

4 shallots, chopped

---

1 tablespoon chopped fresh parsley

1½ oz (40 g) plain flour

---

3 tablespoons double cream

---

4 oz (100 g) fresh white breadcrumbs

Place the scallops in a saucepan with enough wine and water to cover. Add the chopped onion and bouquet garni and season to taste with salt and freshly ground black pepper. Bring to the boil and simmer gently for about 5 minutes or until tender. Strain the scallops, place them in a flameproof serving dish and reserve the liquor.

Melt 2 oz (50 g) of the butter and fry the sliced mushrooms, shallots and parsley for about 3 minutes. Add the flour, cook for about 1 minute, then stir in the liquor from the scallops, stirring continuously until it comes to the boil. Cook for 2 to 3 minutes. Stir in the double cream and pour the sauce over the scallops. Sprinkle with the breadcrumbs, dot with the remaining butter and brown under the grill.

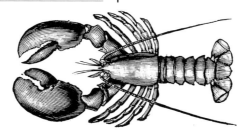

Part Four

MEAT

Beef Olives

Illustrated on page 79

[SERVES 2 TO 3]

I always ask my butcher to cut the steak nice and thin when I am going to cook Beef Olives. It is very difficult to cut it thin enough yourself. This is where it really pays to buy from a craft butcher rather than a supermarket, because you can ask him for exactly what you want. If you are in a hurry, you can use a packet stuffing, but add 2 tablespoons of breadcrumbs to soften the taste. If you want to be really lazy, use gravy granules instead of making your own sauce. Most likely I'll get howled down, but I believe life was given to us to live to the full, with as few complications as possible. They'll come on their own; don't invite them!

1 lb (450 g) topside of beef, cut into thin slices

FOR THE STUFFING:

1 onion, finely chopped

4 oz (100 g) fresh breadcrumbs

1 tablespoon chopped fresh parsley

½ teaspoon chopped fresh thyme

1 tablespoon lemon juice

1 egg, beaten

salt and freshly ground black pepper

FOR THE SAUCE:

1 oz (25 g) unsalted butter

1 large onion, sliced

2 carrots, chopped

1 oz (25 g) flour

1 pint (600 ml) beef stock, thickened with 1 tablespoon beurre manié

Pre-heat the oven to 300°F (150°C), gas mark 2. Place the slices of meat between 2 sheets of greaseproof paper and flatten them with a rolling pin. Cut the meat into pieces about 4 in (10 cm) square. Combine the stuffing ingredients to make a fairly stiff mixture and spread over each piece of meat. Roll up each slice and tuck the ends over to keep the stuffing inside. Using fine string, start at the top and wind the string down each olive, then back to the top and tie securely. Place the beef olives so they fit snugly in a casserole dish.

To make the sauce, melt the butter in a frying pan and fry the onion gently for about 3 minutes until transparent. Add the carrots and fry for a further 3 minutes, then add the flour and cook for 2 minutes. Stir in the beef stock, bring to the boil and simmer for 2 minutes. Pour the boiling gravy over the beef olives just to cover them nicely and place in a slow oven for $2\frac{1}{2}$ to 3 hours.

Roast Rib of Beef

[SERVES 4 TO 6]

I like to use a rib or fore-rib when I roast beef, and I generally roast it on the bone because it tastes sweeter. But many people only want a small piece of beef, and if you are not very good at carving, you may prefer to buy sirloin off the bone. You should allow about 8 oz (225 g) per person on the bone, or about 6 oz (175 g) off the bone. I like the sound of the meat sizzling in the oven while it is cooking; I can always tell that it is cooking well by the sound.

1 rib or fore-rib joint of beef

salt and freshly ground black pepper

Work out your roasting time by allowing 15 minutes per 1 lb (450 g) plus 15 minutes. Roasting must be according to personal taste (a meat thermometer can be a good investment if you are nervous). If you like your beef well done, add 5 minutes per 1 lb (450 g), or if you prefer it rare allow 5 minutes less. The meat should finish cooking 20 minutes before the rest of the meal.

Pre-heat the oven to 425°F (220°C), gas mark 7. Place the meat on a roasting rack in a shallow roasting tin and season with salt and freshly ground black pepper. Place in the oven for 20 minutes to seal the meat, then turn the temperature down to 350°F (180°C), gas mark 4 for the remainder of the roasting time. When cooked, remove the meat from the oven and wrap it in kitchen foil. It will keep hot and be much easier to carve.

My family like to have beef on Christmas Day; we have our turkey at Easter instead. I serve the beef with sprouts and roast potatoes, Yorkshire pudding and mashed or roast parsnips. There are always a lot of us: my daughter Bertha and her husband Richard, my nieces Edna and her friend John, and Sara and her husband Peter, plus my cousin from next door, and anyone else who may otherwise be on their own.

For dessert, we have our mince pies with rum butter (see page 187), then a cheeseboard and fruit salad. It is a much lighter pudding after a heavy lunch, and we save the Christmas pudding for Boxing Day, to follow our cold meat and jacket potatoes. You can buy so many lovely cheeses and biscuits now. I love a Stilton or a strong Cheddar, and a Gloucester, a walnut cheese or Cotswold with chives are particular favourites. Cambozola, a soft blue cheese, is nice, but I have been rather spoiled for Camembert and Brie as they are not the same here as in France; they are always too hard.

Traditional Steak and Kidney Pudding

[SERVES 4 TO 6]

This was a popular lunch dish for servants which we made in *The Victorian Kitchen* television series. I've often made a very large version of this for shooting lunches, using 4 lb (1.75 kg) of meat which, of course, needs cooking for much longer than the small version. It reheats well and is even better the next day. You don't have to use the parsley, but if it is available, I chop the onion and parsley together. I'm noted for using parsley!

12 oz (350 g) plain flour

6 oz (175 g) shredded suet

½ teaspoon salt

½ pint (300 ml) water

1½ lb (750 g) stewing steak, cut into 1 in (2.5 cm) cubes

4–6 oz (100–175 g) beef kidney, cored and trimmed

salt and freshly ground black pepper

1 tablespoon plain flour

1 onion, chopped

1 tablespoon chopped fresh parsley

Mix the flour, suet and salt together, then gradually add the water to make a firm, smooth paste. Roll out two-thirds of the pastry on a floured board and use it to line a greased 2 pint (1.2 litre) pudding basin. Season the meat with salt and freshly ground black pepper and roll it in flour, then lay it in the crust. Scatter over the chopped onion and parsley. Pour in enough cold water to come halfway up the filling. Roll out the remaining pastry to form the cover and seal the pudding by wetting the edges of the pastry and pressing them together. Cover with greased greaseproof paper and tie a pudding cloth over the top. Place the basin in a large saucepan and pour in boiling water to come halfway up the sides of the basin so that it does not splash over on to the pudding. Boil for 3½ hours, topping up with boiling water as necessary. Unwrap the pudding and serve it from the basin with a selection of winter vegetables.

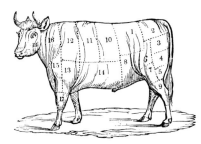

Boeuf Carbonade

[SERVES 4]

I like to cut my meat myself; that way I can take out any fat or gristle and see what I am buying. One old cook told me never to trust butchers or policemen! I like to use thick skirt steak or braising steak, but you can use shin if you are really going to cook slow and long. If you roll it in plenty of flour you should not need any more thickening. If you feel it needs a bit more zip, pop in a spoonful of Bovril or an Oxo cube, or a packet of beef and tomato or mushroom soup, straight from the packet.

2 lb (1 kg) braising steak, cut into finger pieces
2 tablespoons plain flour
2 tablespoons oil
2 onions, sliced
2 carrots, sliced
2 sticks celery, sliced
1 turnip, cubed
salt and freshly ground black pepper
½ pint (300 ml) beer or red wine
½ pint (300 ml) water
1 bouquet garni

Pre-heat the oven to 300°F (150°C), gas mark 2. Roll the steak in the flour. Heat the oil and brown the steak on all sides then put it into a casserole dish. Add the vegetables to the oil and fry until browned, then pop them into the casserole. Season to taste with salt and freshly ground black pepper and cover with beer of your choice, or the remains of the red wine from last night's dinner. Top up with water as required. Add the bouquet garni, cover and put into the oven for a good 3 hours. Check the casserole after 1 hour; if it appears to be cooking too fast, turn the oven down to 275°F (140°C), gas mark 1.

One thing I especially like which we used to cook for the staff in the big houses is silverside of beef. If they were salt, we would soak them overnight before cooking them. We used to put two silversides with some carrots, onions and other vegetables in a big fish kettle and boil them slowly. Suet dumplings went into the pot about half an hour before dishing up; one each for the girls and two for the men. You do not often see large silversides these days, only silly little bits, but a good-sized silverside makes a lovely centrepiece for a buffet at a family party.

Oaty Meatloaf with Quick Tomato Sauce

[SERVES 4]

This quick and easy loaf is a good family meal, and the tomato sauce is simple to make with a tin of chopped tomatoes. Always buy the best quality mince you can for any recipe using mince. My butcher makes my mince specially because he knows I like the highest quality meat.

---

1 lb (450 g) minced beef

---

2 oz (50 g) porridge oats

---

1 egg, beaten

---

1 medium onion, chopped

---

salt and freshly ground black pepper

½ teaspoon thyme (optional)

---

a little water

FOR THE QUICK TOMATO SAUCE:

---

1 × 14 oz (400 g) tin chopped tomatoes

---

1 oz (25 g) flour or arrowroot mixed with 1 tablespoon cold water

---

salt and freshly ground black pepper

---

a pinch of basil

Pre-heat the oven to 350°F (180°C), gas mark 4. Hurtle all the ingredients except the water into a bowl and mix well, including the thyme if you like more flavour. I usually mix by hand: this way you can feel if a little water is required. Turn the mixture into a greased 2 lb (1 kg) loaf tin and bake for about 1 hour.

Meanwhile, make the tomato sauce. Heat the tomatoes in a saucepan. Add about 2 tablespoons of the hot chopped tomatoes to the slaked flour or arrowroot, then return the mixture to the saucepan and bring to the boil, stirring. Season with salt, freshly ground black pepper and a pinch of basil, and add a pinch of sugar if the tomatoes seem a little sharp. Cook for about 3 minutes. If you follow this method you should not end up with blobs in your sauce.

Although a lot of people won't use shallots, I like to cook with them, and you can use them for almost all the recipes using onion. I grow some in amongst the flowers in the garden.

Sara's Meat Roll

Illustrated on page 114

[SERVES 4]

This is a favourite family recipe which my niece Sara first baked at school. You can use the filling to make flan-size patties with left-overs of pastry in 4 in (10 cm) tins, which are lovely cold with salad and ideal for picnics.

For a special occasion, you can plait the pastry over the top of the filling. Roll out the rectangle and very lightly mark it lengthways into thirds. Make diagonal cuts in the outside thirds, cutting up towards the centre strip at about 2 in (5 cm) intervals. Place the filling in the centre third and alternately fold over the strips from one side, then the other, damping the pastry to seal it and finishing off neatly at the end.

FOR THE PASTRY:

2 oz (50 g) hard margarine
2 oz (50 g) lard
6 oz (175 g) strong plain flour
a good pinch of salt
8–9 tablespoons ice cold water

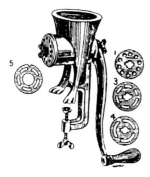

FOR THE FILLING:

4 oz (100 g) sausagemeat
4 oz (100 g) minced beef
1 medium onion, chopped
1 small clove garlic, finely crushed
1 tablespoon tomato purée
1 teaspoon mixed herbs
1 egg, beaten

Pre-heat the oven to 425°F (220°C), gas mark 7. To make the pastry, follow the method for Flaky Pastry on page 200. Roll out the pastry into a rectangle. Reserve a little of the beaten egg for glazing, then place all the filling ingredients in a bowl and mix well. Place the filling in the centre of the pastry, brush the edges with water and bring them up to form a roll, sealing the joins carefully. Place on a greased baking tin. Brush with the remaining beaten egg. Use any left-over bits of pastry to make some leaves to place down the centre of the roll, then brush them with beaten egg. Place in the oven and bake for about 30 minutes until the pastry is golden brown and the meat is cooked.

Veal Goulash

[SERVES 4]

Veal for me is a very bland meat and can be dry if roasted. Also English veal tends to be too pink, no doubt caused by present-day feeding as the calves are not entirely milk-fed any more. So I prefer to casserole it with some spicy ingredients to bring out the flavour and keep the meat moist. You can also make the recipe with pork.

---

1 oz (25 g) lard

---

1 lb (450 g) onions, finely sliced

1½ lb (750 g) shoulder of veal, cut into 2 in (5 cm) cubes

---

1 pint (600 ml) Chicken Stock (see page 198)

1½ tablespoons tomato purée

---

1 tablespoon paprika

---

salt and freshly ground black pepper

---

1 tablespoon arrowroot

---

8 fl oz (250 ml) white wine

¼ pint (150 ml) soured cream or fromage frais

---

a squeeze of lemon juice (optional)

Pre-heat the oven to 300°F (150°C), gas mark 2. Melt the lard in a flameproof casserole and fry the onions until soft but not browned. Put them into a food processor and process until smooth, then return them to the casserole and add the veal, stock, tomato purée and paprika, and season to taste with salt and freshly ground black pepper. Mix well and bring the mixture slowly to the boil. Cover the casserole, and cook it in the oven for about 2 hours until tender. Remove the casserole from the oven.

Mix the arrowroot with a little cold water, then mix in a spoonful of the stock and pour the mixture into the casserole with the white wine. Bring it back to the boil again, then take it off the heat and stir in the soured cream or fromage frais and a squeeze of lemon juice if the taste is not sharp enough. If you add fromage frais, be sure not to let the goulash boil. Serve in a border of boiled rice or soft mashed potato with a green vegetable.

Emmenthal Veal Envelopes

[SERVES 4]

This is a handy dish which can be cooked at the last minute and tastes nice served with a purée of spinach.

4 slices veal cut from the leg, about $\frac{1}{2}$ in (1 cm) thick

2–3 slices ham

4 oz (100 g) Emmenthal or Gruyère cheese

2 tablespoons plain flour, seasoned with salt and freshly ground black pepper

1 egg, beaten

4 oz (100 g) fresh white breadcrumbs

1 oz (25 g) unsalted butter

1 tablespoon oil

With a sharp knife, cut a pocket in the top edge of each slice of veal, then give it a bash to flatten it slightly. Sandwich a slice of cheese between two slices of ham, cut them to size, and fill each pocket with the ham and cheese. Either sew up the opening with fine string (I use white thread) or secure with a cocktail stick. Dust with seasoned flour, dip in beaten egg, then roll in breadcrumbs and put in the fridge for about 1 hour to chill.

Heat the butter and oil in a frying pan and fry the veal envelopes for about 10 minutes until a nice light brown on each side. Drain on kitchen paper and remove the thread or cocktail stick before serving.

Navarin of Lamb

[SERVES 4]

My butcher cuts neck of lamb into cutlets for making navarin. You can use loin, but neck is traditional, tastes good and is less expensive.

---

1 oz (25 g) lard

---

2 lb (1 kg) best end of neck of lamb, cut into cutlets

---

2 tablespoons plain flour, seasoned with salt and freshly ground black pepper

---

1 lb (450 g) carrots, thinly sliced

---

12 baby onions

---

4 oz (100 g) turnip, chopped

---

4 oz (100 g) swede, chopped

---

1 tablespoon plain flour

¾ pint (450 ml) Chicken Stock (see page 198) or made with stock cubes

---

1 tablespoon tomato purée

---

1 bouquet garni

---

salt and freshly ground black pepper

---

1 tablespoon chopped fresh parsley

Pre-heat the oven to 325°F (160°C), gas mark 3. Melt the lard in a frying pan. Coat the cutlets in the seasoned flour and fry in the fat until browned on both sides. Place the cutlets in a large casserole dish and add the vegetables. Add about 1 tablespoon flour to the frying pan and fry gently for 2 minutes, then stir in the stock and tomato purée and bring to the boil. Pour the sauce into the casserole dish and add the bouquet garni. Season to taste with salt and freshly ground black pepper. Cook for about 1½ hours until the vegetables and meat are tender. Remove the bouquet garni and sprinkle with parsley before serving.

Instead of thickening with flour, I sometimes hurtle a packet of soup into a casserole. You can use whatever you fancy, but mushroom is a particular favourite of mine.

Minty Lamb Cutlets

[SERVES 4]

This recipe uses best end of neck of lamb. Steaming the meat helps to keep it moist. It doesn't look as elegant at first, but once it has been cooled and trimmed into cutlets, it looks and tastes wonderful with a chaudfroid sauce and a thin glaze of minted aspic jelly made with a dash of sherry to give it a lovely flavour. You can leave out the chaudfroid sauce for a change, but always make aspic jelly carefully and use only a thin glaze. I have known people make aspic jelly you could sole your shoes with!

---

1 best end of neck of lamb

---

1 onion, quartered

---

2 carrots, thickly sliced

---

4 sprigs mint

---

1 × 1 oz (25 g) sachet aspic powder

½ pint (300 ml) water

¼ pint (150 ml) dry sherry

½ pint (300 ml) Velouté Sauce (see page 195)

---

salt and freshly ground black pepper

Place the lamb, onion and carrots in a saucepan with about 1 pint (600 ml) of water. Bring to the boil, cover and simmer gently for 20 minutes per 1 lb (450 g) plus 20 minutes extra. Remove from the saucepan and leave to cool. Trim off any fat, slice into cutlets and bare about 1½ in (4 cm) of bone at the end of each cutlet. Arrange the cutlets on a serving plate.

Dunk the fresh mint into boiling water for a second, then chop it finely. This will prevent the mint from turning brown. Make up the aspic jelly with the water and sherry, according to the instructions on the sachet. Make the velouté sauce, and stir in ½ pint (300 ml) of aspic jelly. Season to taste with salt and freshly ground black pepper. Pour the sauce over the cutlets and allow to get cold. Mix the chopped mint into the remaining aspic jelly when beginning to set and carefully spoon this thinly over the sauce to give a lovely minted shine.

Roast Lamb with Herb Stuffing

Illustrated on page 74

[SERVES 6 TO 8]

You will have to find a family butcher like mine to prepare the meat for this recipe, or attack it yourself. If you've never done this before, leave yourself plenty of time.

---

1 × 4 lb (1.75 kg) leg of lamb

---

2 tablespoons oil

---

2 medium onions, chopped

---

12 oz (350 g) sausagemeat

---

1 tablespoon chopped fresh parsley

---

1 tablespoon chopped fresh thyme

---

1 teaspoon chopped fresh rosemary

---

salt and freshly ground black pepper

The first requirement when boning meat is a good sharp filleting knife. Start by keeping the knife as close to the bone as possible and work from the top towards the knuckle. If you find you are cutting away too much meat, worry not! Chop it up and put it in the stuffing. Roll the meat back as you go if you can manage it – this way it keeps the stuffing inside better – but you can cheat by cutting the joint along the line of the bone.

Pre-heat the oven to 350°F (180°C), gas mark 4. Heat the oil in a frying pan and fry the onions for about 5 minutes until transparent. Turn them into a bowl and mix in the sausagement and herbs and season to taste with salt and freshly ground black pepper. Push this into the cavity of the meat and sew up the join with fine string. Don't pack the stuffing too tight; if you have a little left over, roll it into balls and place it around the meat for the last 20 minutes of cooking. Place the meat in a roasting tin and roast for about 20 minutes per 1 lb (450 g) plus 20 minutes extra. Don't forget to remove the string before serving.

The old kitchen range burning away
– cleaning it out every morning is something I don't miss one bit!

The secret of good cooking is to have good suppliers – and my butcher's one of the best!

OPPOSITE] *Roast Lamb with Herb Stuffing (page 72); Lamb-Roast Potato and Onion (page 121).*
OVERLEAF] *Pork with Prunes in Red Wine (page 81); Peach-Honey Ham (page 84).*

Beef Olives (page 62).

OPPOSITE] *Pheasant Breasts with Foie Gras (page 104).*

The cottage next door to mine. In the 1930s, when this photograph was taken, almost all the cottages in the village had honeysuckle or beautiful roses around the door.

Lamb with Caper Sauce

[SERVES 4]

This dish always used to be made with mutton, but it can be adapted to lamb. You can use a leg, but I often use loin chops for convenience.

4 loin lamb chops

1 onion, chopped

1 carrot, chopped

1 bouquet garni

½ pint (300 ml) Béchamel Sauce (see page 194) made with the meat juices (see method)

salt and freshly ground black pepper

1 tablespoon capers

a dash of tarragon vinegar (optional)

Pre-heat the oven to 350°F (180°C), gas mark 4. Put the chops, onion, carrot and bouquet garni in a flameproof casserole dish, just cover with water, bring slowly to the boil on top of the cooker, then place in the oven for about 1 hour until cooked. Remove the chops from the casserole and strain and reserve the juice. Make the béchamel sauce using 8 fl oz (250 ml) of the casserole juice with 2 fl oz (50 ml) of milk to make it white. Season to taste with salt and freshly ground black pepper. Stir in the capers; a tablespoonful should be enough to give the sauce a nice sharp flavour, but if you like more sharpness, add a dash of tarragon vinegar.

Pork with Prunes in Red Wine

Illustrated on pages 76–7

[SERVES 4]

You can also use apricots soaked in white wine for this recipe.

8 oz (225 g) prunes, soaked overnight in red wine

1½–2 lb (750 g–1 kg) pork fillet

2 tablespoons plain flour, seasoned with salt and freshly ground black pepper

2 oz (50 g) unsalted butter

2 teaspoons redcurrant jelly

¼ pint (150 ml) single cream

salt and freshly ground black pepper

Place the soaked prunes and wine in a saucepan, bring to the boil and simmer gently for about 30 minutes until tender. Cut the fillet into slices about ½ in (1 cm) thick and dust with seasoned flour. Melt the butter in a frying pan and fry the fillets in the hot butter for about 5 minutes each side, colouring well on both sides. Remove them to a serving dish, arrange the prunes around them and keep them warm. Drain away some of the butter, add the juice from the prunes to the pan, bring to the boil and boil until the liquid has reduced by half. Stir in the redcurrant jelly and cream, season to taste with salt and freshly ground black pepper and boil until the sauce is fairly thick. Pour over the meat and serve with a border of mashed potatoes or rice.

Devilled Pork Chops

[SERVES 4]

The marinade for this recipe has a lovely sharp taste. It can be made when you need it, but I always keep some in an airtight container in the fridge. It also freezes well. It is ideal for grilling or barbecues and can be used on almost any meat, but tastes best on pork or chicken.

---

2 tablespoons oil

4 pork chops or belly pork slices

FOR THE BARBECUE SAUCE:

1 large onion, chopped

1 large clove garlic, crushed

salt and freshly ground black pepper

2 tablespoons mango chutney

1 tablespoon tomato purée

1 teaspoon mustard powder

2 tablespoons Worcestershire sauce

1 tablespoon clear honey

1–2 tablespoons vinegar

Pre-heat the oven to 350°F (180°C), gas mark 4. Heat the oil in a frying pan and fry the pork chops or slices until golden brown on both sides. Remove them from the pan and put them in a roasting tin. Fry the onion and garlic in the oil for about 3 minutes until transparent but not brown. Add all the remaining ingredients, mix well and spoon over the chops. Place in the oven for about 45 minutes until the pork is cooked to your satisfaction, but keep a wary eye on it, as the sweetness of the ingredients makes it catch easily. If this looks like being the case, turn down the heat to 325°F (160°C), gas mark 3 and cook for a little longer.

If I can get a pig's head and trotter from the butcher, I often make brawn. Not many people make it nowadays as it is a bit of a laborious job, so when I do make it I have a job to get a bit for myself. 'If you're making brawn, don't forget I like it!' everyone says. I even spoil Lucy, my old dog, by giving her a bit.

Crackly Roast Pork

[SERVES 8 TO 10]

I think it is worthwhile to mention roast pork. It's not often these days that a whole leg or loin is a Sunday lunch (we tend to have smaller joints), but it is worth knowing how to cook it properly, whatever the size, to get the crackling crisp. This is sometimes difficult today as the skin is so tender with the modern farming methods, but it is possible and is a lovely accompaniment to the meat.

1 leg or loin joint of pork

salt

oil

a sprig of rosemary

1 large onion, sliced

1 sharp apple, cored and sliced

Pre-heat the oven to 425°F (220°C), gas mark 7. Work out your roasting time which should allow 25 minutes per 1 lb (450 g) plus 25 minutes. There are 3 ways to prepare the crackling to make it crisp and everyone has their own favourite. You can rub on some salt, rub on oil and salt or take pot luck. Whichever you choose, it is essential to pre-heat the oven so that it is really hot when you put in the pork. Roast for 20 minutes, then reduce the temperature to 375°F (190°C), gas mark 5 for the remaining cooking time. Keep an eye on the oven, and as soon as the crackling is nice and brown, lift it off the meat and put it aside. Then you can turn legs of pork over and cook from all sides. Keep your husband out of the kitchen otherwise the crackling will get less on each visit! Place the rosemary, onion and apple underneath the meat, and return it to the oven to finish cooking. Keep the meat well basted. Return the crackling to the oven to heat through before serving.

Peach-Honey Ham

Illustrated on page 76

[SERVES 4 TO 6]

In the old days when we used to buy whole York hams, we bought them dry and they had to be soaked for 3 days. I often had the job of scrubbing them with a scrubbing brush which was a really messy job. It is a lot easier now!

I don't usually bake my ham, I find it gets too dry. I always boil it, then finish it off in the oven. Although many people buy ready-cooked ham, cooking it yourself usually makes it slightly more juicy. I prefer ham on the bone, but you can use this method for any ham joint – on the bone or boned and rolled. My favourite is still York ham; it is lovely and smoky although it can be a bit dry, but boy is it expensive!

There are plenty of variations to this cooking method. You can use pineapple instead of peaches, use dry cider, or simply pat the boiled ham with plenty of demerara sugar and stud with cloves before finishing it off in the oven.

1 × 4 lb (1.75 kg) gammon joint

1 onion, quartered

1 carrot, sliced

1 bay leaf

1 × 14 oz (400 g) tin peaches, drained and juice reserved

2 tablespoons clear honey

12 cloves

Soak the gammon joint in water for 2 to 3 hours to remove any excess salt. Place the joint in a saucepan just large enough to fit, cover with cold water and add the onion, carrot and bay leaf. Bring to the boil and simmer very gently for 25 minutes per 1 lb (450 g) plus 25 minutes extra.

Pre-heat the oven to 400°F (200°C), gas mark 6. Remove the ham from the saucepan and drain it. Peel off the skin, leaving just a small amount of fat. Place the ham in a roasting tin. If you are serving the ham hot, arrange the peaches round it. Mix the honey into $\frac{1}{2}$ pint (300 ml) of the reserved juice and pour this over the ham. Dot the ham with the cloves and put it in the oven for about 15 minutes to brown, basting occasionally with the peach juice. If serving the ham cold, decorate it with the peaches when cool.

I seldom fry or grill meat, particularly pork, which can dry out. In the oven, it not only does not dry out but you don't have to stand over it and watch how it is cooking. I always seal meat in a hot oven, then turn down the temperature, slightly lower for pork than other meats as it is best cooked slowly and must be well cooked. I often make the left-overs into a curry. Sometimes my butcher has a pig from a local man who 'grows his own', and he always saves me a leg. The taste is so different; it does not have the tough fibre of so much pork these days.

Herbed Ham Slice

[SERVES 4]

We used to serve this as a breakfast dish, but it makes an equally good brunch or lunch, or even an appetiser for a main meal. You can vary the herbs, and it is a good way to use all the left-over bits of ham on the shank and bone.

---

1 pint (600 ml) milk

1 oz (25 g) unsalted butter

2 eggs, beaten

2 egg yolks, beaten

1 tablespoon chopped fresh parsley

½ teaspoon chopped fresh thyme

salt and freshly ground black pepper

12 oz (350 g) cooked ham, chopped

Pre-heat the oven to 350°F (180°C), gas mark 4. Place the milk and butter in a saucepan and bring almost to the boil, then remove from the heat. Allow to cool slightly, then pour the milk over the beaten eggs and egg yolks, mix in the herbs and season to taste with salt and freshly ground black pepper. Place the ham in a 1½ pint (900 ml) pie dish. Stir and strain the egg mixture over the ham so that it is well covered but not drowned. Set the pie dish in a baking tin and pour about 1 in (2.5 cm) of cold water into the tin, taking care not to splash any water into the pie dish. Bake for about 35 minutes until the custard is set and the top is golden brown. Serve warm or cold.

Fried Liver with Pernod

[SERVES 4]

Calves' liver is nice for this recipe, but it is expensive so I often use lambs' liver instead. It is very simple to prepare but unusual and delicious. If you feel the Pernod by itself is too strong, add a little cream.

---

1 lb (450 g) calves' or lambs' liver, trimmed and sliced in ¼ in (5 mm) slices

2 tablespoons plain flour, seasoned with salt and freshly ground black pepper

4 oz (100 g) unsalted butter

¼ pint (150 ml) Pernod

8 rashers streaky bacon

Coat the liver in the seasoned flour. Melt the butter in a frying pan, add the liver and fry gently for about 5 minutes, then turn the liver over and fry for a further 3 minutes until the liver is just cooked through. Remove the liver to a serving dish. Pour the Pernod into the pan and bring to the boil, stirring, to collect all the meat juices. Pour over the liver. Meanwhile, grill the bacon until crisp and serve with the liver.

Mushroom Kidneys Turbigo

[SERVES 4]

I like to serve lambs' kidneys but they must be fresh so that they are nice and firm and easy to handle. This is another recipe which includes parsley which I use by the bunch. I grow it in the garden as I use so much. Although some people keep it in a vase of water, I find it keeps much better if you wash and pat it dry, then keep it in a screw-top jar in the fridge. It freezes well too, so if I have any extra I chop it and freeze it in plastic freezer containers.

Melt the butter in a frying or sauté pan and fry the kidneys gently until just browned. Remove the kidneys and fry the mushrooms and onion gently for about 10 minutes. Stir in the flour and cook for 1 to 2 minutes. Gradually stir in the sherry and parsley and season to taste with salt and freshly ground black pepper. Cook for a further 5 minutes. Stir in the cream, add the kidneys and re-heat. Don't overcook the kidneys or they will go hard. Garnish with a sprig of parsley and serve in a circle of rice with broccoli or another green vegetable.

2 oz (50 g) unsalted butter

12 lambs' kidneys, cored and sliced

6 oz (175 g) mushrooms, sliced

1 onion, chopped

1 oz (25 g) plain flour

½ pint (300 ml) dry sherry

1 tablespoon chopped fresh parsley

salt and freshly ground black pepper

¼ pint (150 ml) double cream

a sprig of parsley to garnish

I always use fresh breadcrumbs, never packets, but it is much easier if you always have some handy. I process some bread in the food processor, then spread the breadcrumbs out on kitchen roll to dry for an hour or so, or overnight. Then I put them in an air-tight container and keep them in the fridge, or freeze them. You can do the same with grated cheese.

Casseroled Hearts with Herb Stuffing

[SERVES 4]

Lambs' or pigs' hearts are the best for stuffing, and they need to be cooked slowly so that they are tender.

4 lambs' or pigs' hearts

4 oz (100 g) unsalted butter

1 onion, chopped

2 oz (50 g) fresh white breadcrumbs

1 tablespoon chopped fresh parsley

1 teaspoon chopped fresh thyme

1 egg, beaten

salt and freshly ground black pepper

2 onions, sliced

1 stick celery, sliced

2 carrots, sliced

1 oz (25 g) plain flour

1 pint (600 ml) beef stock

Soak the hearts in cold salt water in the fridge for 2 to 3 hours or overnight; this helps to remove the blood. Pre-heat the oven to 300°F (150°C), gas mark 2. Cut out the pieces of tough skin and tubes, wash the hearts and dry them well. Melt 1 oz (25 g) of the butter in a frying pan and gently fry the chopped onion for about 3 minutes until softened. Add the fried onion to the breadcrumbs, parsley, thyme and egg, season to taste with salt and freshly ground black pepper and mix well. Press the stuffing into the cavities. Melt the remaining butter in a frying pan and brown the hearts all round, then remove them from the pan with a slotted spoon. Gently fry the sliced onions, celery and carrots for about 5 minutes, then remove them from the pan with a slotted spoon and place them in a casserole dish just large enough to hold the hearts. Lay the hearts on top. Put the flour in the frying pan and cook for 2 minutes until it begins to brown. Add the stock and bring to the boil, stirring, then cook for 3 minutes until thickened. Pour the gravy over the hearts and put into the oven for 2 to $2\frac{1}{2}$ hours until tender.

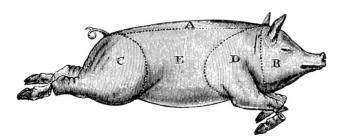

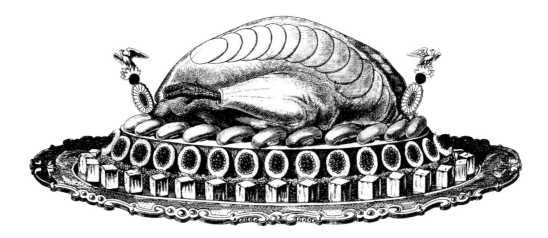

Part Five

POULTRY AND GAME

Spicy Chicken Pie

[SERVES 6 TO 8]

Chicken pies such as this were often served for lunch or at picnics. Sometimes, the bones were left in, but if you bone the chickens, then the pie can be served hot with gravy or sliced and eaten cold as a nice supper dish. Use frozen pastry if you do not wish to make your own.

1 × 4 lb (1.75 kg) chicken, or 2 smaller chickens
1 onion, quartered
2 carrots
1 bouquet garni
6 slices ham, chopped
1 lb (450 g) sausagemeat
3 hard-boiled eggs, halved
½ teaspoon mace
½ teaspoon nutmeg
salt and freshly ground black pepper
8 oz (225 g) Puff Pastry (see page 201) to serve hot or 8 oz (225 g) Flaky Pastry (see page 200) to serve cold
1 egg, beaten

Skin, bone and joint the chicken. Put the bones in a large saucepan with the onion, carrots and bouquet garni, cover with cold water, bring to the boil and simmer for about 1 hour. Strain and discard the bones and vegetables; keep the liquor for the gravy.

Pre-heat the oven to 400°F (200°C) gas mark 6. Put a layer of chicken meat at the bottom of a large greased pie dish, then a layer of ham, then one of sausagemeat and hard-boiled egg halves. Season each layer with a little mace, nutmeg, salt and freshly ground black pepper. Carry on layering until the dish is full. Pour in the cold stock to come about halfway up the filling. Roll out the pastry and cut a cover the size of the dish. Use the trimmings to cut a strip about 1 in (2.5 cm) wide to go round the dish, and some leaves or decorations for the top. Moisten the edge of the dish and press the strip all round, then moisten the pastry strip and seal on the pastry lid. Brush with beaten egg, decorate with the pastry leaves and glaze them with beaten egg. Make 2 holes for the steam to escape. Bake the pie in the oven for about 1 hour, then lower the temperature to 325°F (160°C), gas mark 3 for about another 1 hour until the meat is tender. Cover with a piece of greaseproof paper if the pastry appears to be too brown.

Chicken with Lemon and Tarragon

[SERVES 4]

This recipe has a nice sharp taste to the sauce; it is good served with a border of boiled rice. Before you chop the tarragon, put it in a bowl and cover it with boiling water for a few seconds. This makes it a nice green and pulls out the flavour.

1 chicken

1 onion, quartered

1 carrot

a sprig of tarragon

1 pint (600 ml) Béchamel Sauce (see page 194) made with the cooking liquor

4 tablespoons single or double cream

1 tablespoon lemon juice

1 tablespoon chopped fresh tarragon

1 tablespoon chopped fresh parsley

Put the chicken into a saucepan which is not too large, with the onion, carrot and tarragon. Fill with water to come about halfway up the leg, bring to the boil, then simmer for about $1\frac{1}{2}$ hours until the meat comes off the bone. When the meat is cooked, remove the chicken from the stock to cool. When it is cool enough to handle, remove the meat from the bones. Strain the liquor and use it to make a béchamel sauce, then thin the sauce with just enough cream to make it velvety. Add the chicken meat to the sauce with enough lemon juice to give it a sharp taste. Stir in the tarragon and parsley and serve with boiled rice.

Good-class shops in little places are difficult to find nowadays because the supermarkets have taken away so much trade. But the larger shops don't sell the little delicacies that these little shops could; you have to go to London or the major cities to find specialist shops.

Before the War we used to buy cocks' combs in jars about the size of a half-pint tumbler. They were white, although I don't know if that was because they were skinned or because of the way they were prepared. We used to blanch them to heat them through and put them round Coq au Vin with little triangles of fried bread.

White Devil

[SERVES 4]

There are two versions of this delicious dish which is ideal for using up oddments of cooked chicken or game. The first version is best if you have small pieces of meat, whereas the second is ideal for cooked chicken pieces, larger pieces of cooked game or lamb. When you season the dish, be careful with the salt, as the soy sauce may make it salt enough.

VARIATION 1:

½ pint (300 ml) double or whipping cream, lightly whipped

1 scant tablespoon French mustard

1 tablespoon light soy sauce

1 tablespoon Worcestershire sauce

salt and freshly ground black pepper

12 oz (350 g) cooked chicken

VARIATION 2:

4 pieces cooked chicken, game or lamb

1½ tablespoons French mustard

1 teaspoon white wine vinegar

½ teaspoon light soy sauce

½ teaspoon Worcestershire sauce

½ pint (300 ml) double or whipping cream, lightly whipped

salt and freshly ground black pepper

For Variation 1, pre-heat the oven to 400°F (200°C), gas mark 6. Mix together the cream, mustard, soy sauce and Worcestershire sauce. Season to taste with salt and freshly ground black pepper. Pour the sauce over the chicken in a gratin dish and pop into the hot oven for about 10 minutes until heated through.

For Variation 2, pre-heat the oven to 400°F (200°C), gas mark 6. Place the meat in a gratin dish and heat through in the oven for about 5 minutes. Spread about 1 tablespoon of mustard over the pieces of meat. Mix the remaining mustard with the vinegar, soy sauce and Worcestershire sauce, and add this to the whipped cream. Season to taste with salt and freshly ground black pepper. Mix well and pour over the chicken. Return to the oven for about 5 minutes to brown.

Chicken Broccoli Surprise

Illustrated on page 116

[SERVES 4]

When I was young, every back yard had chickens, and poaching was a good way to cook them, especially for a pie or to eat cold. It is easy to do, and keeps the flesh lovely and moist. The ingredients are not exact, because I just use any odds and ends of vegetables I have available. It goes very well with the broccoli in this recipe.

---

1 × 3 lb (1.5 kg) chicken, poached (see method)

---

2 carrots, roughly sliced

---

1 onion, quartered

---

a few outside sticks celery

---

12 oz (350 g) broccoli, trimmed

---

1 × 15 oz (425 g) tin chicken soup

---

1 teaspoon lemon juice

---

1 teaspoon curry powder

---

4 oz (100 g) fresh white breadcrumbs

---

2 oz (50 g) Cheddar cheese, grated

---

salt and freshly ground black pepper

---

3 tablespoons Creamy Mayonnaise (see page 197)

To poach the chicken, place it in a saucepan just a little bigger than the bird. Add a few carrots, an onion, a few sticks of celery or pieces of celeriac or other vegetables. Fill the saucepan with water to come halfway up the thigh, bring to the boil, then cover the saucepan and simmer for about $1\frac{1}{2}$ hours until the meat is cooked.

Pre-heat the oven to 350°F (180°C), gas mark 4. Cook the broccoli in boiling salted water for about 10 minutes until just tender, then drain it and arrange it in the bottom of a gratin dish. Remove the chicken meat from the bones, cut it into pieces and arrange it over the broccoli. Combine the remaining ingredients in a bowl, adding just enough mayonnaise to make a very soft consistency. Spread the sauce over the chicken, cover with foil and bake for 35 to 45 minutes.

Coq au Vin

[SERVES 4]

This makes a lovely lunch or dinner party dish, especially as you can prepare it either partly or completely in advance. Serve it with fried bread triangles, nice and crunchy, and remember, the better the brandy and red wine, the better the final dish. You can add more red wine if you wish, and include the chicken stock if you like plenty of juice.

Years of experience of cooking have taught me how to do things the easy way, and this includes making as little washing up as possible. I always make dishes like this in a flameproof casserole so that you can do almost everything in the one dish. It is worth investing in a good quality casserole for the amount of work it saves.

---

1 oz (25 g) unsalted butter

---

1 tablespoon olive oil

---

4 oz (100 g) streaky bacon, cut into small strips

---

8 oz (225 g) button mushrooms

---

12 tiny onions

---

1 chicken, cut into serving-sized pieces or 4 chicken breasts or thighs

---

3 tablespoons plain flour, seasoned with salt and freshly ground black pepper

---

2 cloves garlic, crushed

---

1 bouquet garni

½–¾ pint (300–450 ml) Chicken Stock (see page 198)

---

4 tablespoons brandy

½ bottle red wine

---

1 oz (25 g) unsalted butter, softened

Pre-heat the oven to 350°F (180°C), gas mark 4. Heat the butter and oil in a flameproof casserole, add the bacon, and when it begins to turn golden, add the mushrooms and onions. Continue to cook until the onions are transparent and the mushrooms brown, then remove them from the casserole. Roll the chicken pieces in 2 tablespoons of seasoned flour and sauté them in the same fat until golden all over. Return the vegetables to the pan, and add the crushed garlic, bouquet garni and chicken stock. Cover and cook in the oven for about 1 hour until almost cooked.

Remove the casserole from the oven, take out all but the juices and discard the bouquet garni. Warm the brandy in a small pan, ignite it and allow it to burn for a few seconds, then put out the flame with the red wine. Set the casserole on a high heat, add the brandy and wine. Bring to the boil, and allow to reduce to almost half the quantity. Mix the butter and remaining flour together on a plate. Dip a whisk into the roux and whisk it into the juices in small knobs until the sauce thickens. Return the chicken and vegetables to the sauce to heat through. I like triangles of fried bread with this; it's nice and crunchy.

Chicken Maryland with Sweetcorn Pancakes

[SERVES 4]

Chicken Maryland is one of my favourite dishes; it has such a lovely piquant flavour, and is nice served with horseradish sauce. Marinating the chicken in lemon juice before cooking makes the fibres break down and whitens the flesh. It is a lovely dish to make for guests, but it is a last-minute cooking job so it won't wait for them. Also, do not attempt to make it for more than six people – you won't have enough hands to go round.

4 chicken breasts, skinned

juice of 1 lemon

2 tablespoons plain flour, seasoned with salt and freshly ground black pepper

1 egg, beaten

4 oz (100 g) fresh white breadcrumbs

4 tablespoons oil

3 oz (75 g) unsalted butter

8 rashers streaky bacon

12 cocktail sausages

4 bananas

4 tomatoes, halved, or 8 cherry tomatoes, skinned

FOR THE SWEETCORN PANCAKES:

1 × 10½ oz (285 g) tin creamed sweetcorn

2 oz (50 g) plain flour

1 egg, beaten

a little milk

salt and freshly ground black pepper

oil for frying

watercress to garnish

Give the chicken breasts a good bang with a rolling pin to flatten them, as they then cook more quickly. Put them in a bowl, cover them with the lemon juice and leave to soak for at least 2 hours, turning 3 or 4 times. Dry the chicken and roll it in the seasoned flour, then the egg, then the breadcrumbs. Heat the oil and 2 oz (50 g) of butter in a large frying pan and fry the chicken for about 25 minutes until cooked through and golden brown on both sides.

Roll up the bacon and put it on to skewers, then grill it until crispy. Grill the sausages. Cut the bananas in half lengthways and fry them gently in the remaining butter until soft and brown. Garnish with the tomatoes.

To make the sweetcorn pancakes, mix the sweetcorn and flour and beat in the egg with enough milk to make a soft dropping consistency. Season with salt and freshly ground black pepper. Heat a little oil in a frying pan. Drop tablespoonfuls of the batter into the shallow fat and fry for a few minutes until golden brown on both sides.

Assemble all the ingredients on a serving dish, decorate with watercress and serve immediately.

Galantine

Illustrated on page 113

[SERVES 4 TO 6]

This takes a little time, but makes a lovely cold dish as a centrepiece for a buffet. You can adapt the recipe to suit your own taste, using veal or pork and more or less sausagemeat. We made the recipe for *The Victorian Kitchen* television series, and had so many requests for the recipe that we had to print an information sheet!

---

1 large chicken

---

1 onion, quartered

1–2 carrots, sliced

---

8 oz (225 g) sausagemeat

---

3 tablespoons fresh breadcrumbs

½ pint (300 ml) Béchamel Sauce, fairly stiff (see page 194)

---

1 egg, beaten

---

1 onion, chopped

---

1 tablespoon chopped fresh parsley ⎱ *or herbs*
½ teaspoon chopped fresh thyme ⎰ *to taste*

---

salt and freshly ground black pepper

---

6 × ¾ in (2 cm) strips of ham or tongue

---

2 hard-boiled eggs

---

1 × 1 oz (25 g) sachet aspic powder

½ pint (300 ml) water

¼ pint (150 ml) dry sherry

Slit the chicken skin from the back of the neck to the tail. Skin the chicken, keeping the skin in one piece, and remove all the meat from the carcass. Put the bones in a large saucepan, add the onion and carrots, cover with cold water, bring to the boil and simmer for 1½ hours to make the stock. Strain and discard the bones and vegetables.

Mince or process the chicken meat until it is as smooth as required. Mix with the sausagemeat, breadcrumbs, béchamel sauce, beaten egg, chopped onion, parsley and thyme and season to taste with salt and freshly ground black pepper. Open out the chicken skin on a clean cloth. Spread with half the meat mixture about ¾ in (2 cm) thick to within ½ in (1 cm) of the edges. Lay the strips of ham or tongue across the mixture, then cover with the remaining stuffing. Place the hard-boiled eggs in the centre. Bring the two sides over the eggs, keeping them as central as possible, forming a roll. Wrap the cloth round and sew up tightly. Tie both ends of the cloth. Place the galantine in the stock, making sure that it is well covered, bring to the boil and simmer for about 2½ hours.

Remove from the heat. When nearly cool, take out the galantine and tighten up the cloth. Place the galantine between 2 dishes with weights on top until it is cold. Remove the cloth and trim the edges. Dissolve the aspic in the water and sherry according to the instructions on the sachet and spoon a thin glaze over the galantine to finish. Serve in thick slices, with salad.

Chicken Paprika

[SERVES 4]

The rich red colour of this dish looks very pretty served with noodles, white or green, and tastes delicious.

---

1 large chicken or 4 chicken pieces

---

2 tablespoons plain flour

---

4 oz (100 g) unsalted butter

---

1 large onion, chopped

---

1 oz (25 g) paprika

---

8 oz (225 g) tomatoes, skinned, deseeded and chopped

---

1 tablespoon tomato purée

---

salt and freshly ground black pepper

½ pint (300 ml) water or Chicken Stock (see page 198), warmed

---

1 bay leaf

---

4 outside sticks celery, chopped

---

1 clove garlic, crushed

¼ pint (150 ml) cream

---

1 squeeze lemon juice (optional)

Pre-heat the oven to 400°F (200°C), gas mark 6. Cut the chicken into about 8 portions and rub each piece in flour. Melt 2 oz (50 g) of the butter in a frying pan and fry the chicken for a few minutes until golden. Transfer it to a roasting tin with the fat and roast it in the oven for 20 to 30 minutes, keeping the chicken well basted.

To make the sauce, melt the remaining butter in a saucepan, add the onion and fry it gently until soft and golden. Sprinkle on the paprika, add the tomatoes and tomato purée and cook for about 5 minutes, stirring well. Season to taste with salt and freshly ground black pepper. Add the water or stock, bay leaf, celery and garlic, bring to the boil, cover and simmer gently for about 20 minutes until cooked. Remove the bay leaf, pour the sauce into a food processor and process until smooth. Return the sauce to the saucepan, add the cooked chicken and heat through gently. Stir in the cream, but do not let the sauce boil. Add a squeeze of lemon juice if the sauce is not sharp enough. Serve with white or green noodles.

Chicken Spring Mousse

[SERVES 4]

This makes a lovely summer dish to serve with a mixed green salad.

---

12 oz (350 g) cold cooked chicken

---

1 × ½ oz (15 g) sachet gelatine powder

---

4 tablespoons Chicken Stock (see page 198)

½ pint (300 ml) double or whipping cream, lightly whipped

---

salt and freshly ground black pepper

---

1 tablespoon horseradish or Worcestershire sauce

---

1 × 1 oz (25 g) sachet aspic powder

---

1 tomato, sliced

---

1 hard-boiled egg, sliced

Chop or process the chicken, but not too finely. Soak the gelatine in the chicken stock, warm it to dissolve it completely, then add it to the meat when beginning to set. Fold in the lightly whipped cream and the chicken, and season to taste with salt and freshly ground black pepper. Stir in enough horseradish or Worcestershire sauce to give a piquant taste. Turn the mixture into a soufflé dish and leave in the fridge to set. Make up the aspic according to the instructions on the sachet. When it is almost cold, spoon a thin layer over the mousse. Decorate the top with slices of tomato and rounds of hard-boiled egg, leave to set, then spoon over another covering of aspic to glaze.

Brandy and Tarragon Poussins

Illustrated on page 117

[SERVES 4]

Poussins can be a bit flavourless at some times of the year, so wait until you see them fresh in the shops rather than buying them frozen. You can serve them with mashed potato and a nice green vegetable.

---

4 poussins

---

4 sprigs of tarragon

---

4 oz (100 g) unsalted butter

---

2 tablespoons oil

---

4 slices bread

---

8 oz (100 g) mushrooms, sliced

½ pint (300 ml) cream

2–3 tablespoons brandy

Pre-heat the oven to 400°F (200°C), gas mark 6. Wipe the poussins so they are nice and dry inside and pop in a piece of tarragon and a knob of butter. Melt the remaining butter and brush all over the poussins. Place them in a roasting tin and roast in the oven, basting frequently, for about 45 minutes until cooked through and tender. Heat the oil in a frying pan and fry the bread until crisp. Arrange on a serving dish. Remove the poussins to the serving dish. Bring the meat juices to the boil, add the mushrooms, cream and brandy and simmer for a few minutes, stirring well. Spoon the sauce over the poussins and serve immediately.

Smoked Chicken Mayonnaise

[SERVES 4]

Smoked chicken makes a lovely light lunch on a hot day, ideal if your family have requested a sticky treacle pudding for afters, as mine often do! My butcher gets my chicken smoked for me – long live the village butcher! I am afraid we are eventually going to come to the state where we have nothing but pre-packaged meat as there are so few real old-fashioned butchers about now. If you have one, do use him! Apart from the speed and convenience of supermarket shopping, I wonder if the decline of the butchers is not something to do with the fact that we buy small pieces of meat nowadays. When I was at school, it was not unusual for there to be eight or nine people in a family so they needed big lumps of meat. It may not have been sirloin, but perhaps a big piece of brisket, which the mother would know how to prepare and, since she was at home, could pop into the oven for a long slow cook.

---

1 smoked chicken, chopped into large pieces

---

2 spring onions (or to taste), finely chopped

½ pint (300 ml) Creamy Mayonnaise (see page 197), thinned to coating consistency with double cream or fromage frais

---

salt and freshly ground black pepper

---

1 avocado pear, sliced

---

a few drops of lemon juice

Mix the chicken and spring onions into the mayonnaise and season with salt and freshly ground black pepper. At the last minute, slice the avocado and arrange it on top. Squeeze a few drops of lemon juice over the avocado to stop it discolouring. Serve with a mixed green salad.

I believe smoked chicken is becoming more readily available, but if you have difficulty getting hold of it, contact the following organisation for the address of your nearest supplier:

*Juliette Evans, Chief Executive,
Delicatessen and Fine Foods Association,
6 The Broadway,
Thatcham,
Berkshire
RG13 4JA.
(Tel: 0635 69033.)*

Chicken Liver Risotto

[SERVES 4]

Have a look in the fridge before you start this quick dish, as you can use up the odd sausage, slice of ham or bacon. I like to use brown rice; it gives a nicer look. Some people cook white rice until it's all thick and stodgy, like 'Chinese wedding cake' – an army phrase!

2 oz (50 g) unsalted butter
1 onion, finely chopped or sliced
4 oz (100 g) mushrooms, sliced
6 oz (175 g) long-grain brown rice
1 pint (600 ml) Chicken Stock (see page 198)
12 oz (350 g) chicken livers
1 tablespoon chopped fresh parsley
2 oz (50 g) Parmesan cheese, grated

Melt 1 oz (25 g) of the butter in a large saucepan or wok, add the onion and cook for about 3 minutes until soft but not browned. Add the mushrooms and cook for a further 5 minutes. Add the rice and stir the ingredients together for about 2 minutes so that the rice is covered with fat. Take the pan off the heat and add the stock, then cover the pan and return it to the heat to simmer gently for about 15 minutes until the rice is tender and the liquid is absorbed.

While the rice is cooking, melt the remaining butter in another frying pan, add the chicken livers and cook for about 10 minutes. Mix the chicken livers into the rice, add the chopped parsley and sprinkle with Parmesan cheese. Serve immediately.

I worked at Basildon House for 18 years, but I lived at home then. I started early in the morning and came home in the afternoon, going back in the evening if the family was at home. It was not so busy during the week, but we always had house guests from Friday afternoon until Sunday after lunch, plus lots of visitors coming and going. We used to prepare breakfast and lunch, then leave a tea of cakes or sandwiches and scones for the afternoon. Then we would come back and prepare dinner. Dinner parties on Saturday were for at least 12, often 20 people. Monday I called my clearing-up day because we would use up what was in the fridge and sometimes I'd go through the menus with Lady Iliffe, but sometimes she would just leave it to me. Then I'd have a cake-making day to fill up the tins for the weekend, and Thursday was shopping day, because I don't like to go out shopping on the day when I am preparing food for a dinner.

Turkey Legs with Chestnut or Mushroom Stuffing

[SERVES 4]

I always take the turkey legs off the bird before cooking. If you do this carefully, the breast is not cut into. This way the bird cooks in less time – and both gas and electricity seem to take a downward trend when everyone is cooking their Christmas bird! When left on, the legs always seem to be left to go dry and are not enjoyed as they should be. You can cook the legs on Christmas Day and carve them with the breast, or serve them cold on Boxing Day. Or you can freeze them as they are, make them into a casserole, or stuff them to make a rather different and special meal.

By the way, always make sure your turkey finishes roasting half an hour before lunch. Wrap it in kitchen foil – it will keep hot enough and will carve much better.

---

2 turkey legs, boned

FOR A CHESTNUT STUFFING:

8 oz (225 g) pork sausagemeat

---

2 oz (50 g) fresh white breadcrumbs

---

1 egg, beaten

---

8 oz (225 g) chestnuts, peeled, cooked and finely chopped or puréed,
or 1 × 8 oz (225 g) tin chestnut purée

---

a pinch of mace

---

1 tablespoon sherry or brandy

---

salt and freshly ground black pepper

FOR A MUSHROOM STUFFING:

8 oz (225 g) pork sausagemeat

---

1 egg, beaten

---

4 oz (100 g) mushrooms, chopped

---

3 tablespoons cream

---

2 teaspoons chopped fresh parsley

---

6 tablespoons white wine

---

salt and freshly ground black pepper

Pre-heat the oven to 400°F (200°C), gas mark 6. Mix together all the ingredients for your chosen stuffing. Cut the turkey meat into 4 pieces, fill each one with stuffing and tie round into a roll with string. Place in a roasting tin and roast for about 50 minutes until cooked through and tender.

An easy and tasty way to cook turkey legs is to mix a teaspoonful of curry powder into 2 oz (50 g) of softened butter. Push this under the skin, brush melted butter over the legs, wrap in foil and bake until thoroughly cooked, then open the foil and allow the legs to brown.

Duck with Apricots and Brandy

[SERVES 4]

I used to love the great big Aylesbury ducks, but you can't buy them any more. A cook was always considered a very good carver if he could get enough for five people off an Aylesbury duck. You can use tinned apricots for this recipe, but make sure they are in natural juice not syrup, and drain them well before you start. Serve the duck with mashed or boiled potatoes and a green salad.

---

1 duck

---

4 oz (100 g) unsalted butter

---

1 tablespoon olive oil

½ pint (300 ml) Chicken Stock (see page 198)

¼ pint (150 ml) medium dry white wine

---

1 lb (450 g) fresh apricots, halved and stones removed

---

1 tablespoon orange juice

---

3 tablespoons brandy

Pre-heat the oven to 325°F (160°C), gas mark 3. Prick the duck skin in 1 or 2 places without stabbing the flesh. Heat the butter and oil in a frying pan or roasting tin and brown the duck on all sides. Put the duck in a flameproof casserole. Cover with the stock and wine, bring to the boil, cover and cook in the oven for 1½ to 2 hours. Add half the apricot halves to the pan after 40 minutes.

When the duck is cooked, lift it on to a serving dish, arrange the remaining apricot halves round the duck and keep it warm. Strain the cooking liquid and skim off the fat. Bring the liquid to the boil and boil until it is reduced by one-third. Sieve or process the cooked apricots until smooth, then add them to the sauce with the orange juice. Re-heat and pour into a sauce boat. Warm the brandy in a small pan, then pour it over the duck and set it alight to serve.

Roast Goose with Apple Stuffing

[SERVES 6 TO 8]

Years ago the goose was always a Michaelmas dish, now it doesn't feature very much, though sometimes turns up at Christmas instead of turkey. It is quite a greasy bird so requires no fat, and needs the skin stabbing before cooking, but make sure you don't pierce the flesh.

If you really want to take a step back in time, keep the fat that runs from the bird and rub it on your chest when you've got a nasty cough (hardly Chanel No. 5!).

I seldom do anything to goose, turkey or duck other than put an apple or onion in the cavity. Stuffing makes the bird take much longer to cook and also tends to make the bird go 'off' quicker. Use this unusual stuffing to cook round the goose.

---

1 × 6 lb (2.75 kg) goose

---

1 apple or onion

FOR THE STUFFING:

---

8 oz (225 g) dried prunes, stoned

---

2 oz (50 g) raisins

---

4 oz (100 g) fresh white breadcrumbs

---

2 oz (50 g) shredded suet

---

1 large apple, peeled, cored and chopped

---

salt and freshly ground black pepper

---

1 egg, beaten

Pre-heat the oven to 400°F (200°C), gas mark 6. Wash and dry the goose and place the apple or onion in the cavity. Place the bird in a roasting tin and cover loosely with foil. Roast in the oven for 15 minutes per 1 lb (450 g) plus 15 minutes. Remove the foil for the last 45 minutes of cooking to allow the skin to brown.

To make the stuffing, put the prunes and raisins in a bowl and cover with boiling water. Leave them to stand for about 5 minutes, then drain and chop them. Mix in the breadcrumbs, suet and apple and season to taste with salt and freshly ground black pepper. Bind the stuffing together with the egg. Make the stuffing into balls and place them round the goose for the last 45 minutes of cooking.

Never do a recipe for the first time and expect to serve it to guests; try it first. I would not attempt to do a recipe for a party if I had not made it before. That is where things start to go wrong! If you have made it yourself you know whether it needs an extra five minutes in the oven, for example, or a little more seasoning.

Pheasant Breasts with Foie Gras

Illustrated on page 78

[SERVES 4]

Don't stint on anything with this recipe. It is a wonderful dish, very expensive, for the most special occasions. I only saw the dish made twice, for dinner parties for about 12 or 18 people. It was such a delightful taste I've never forgotten it. Real *foie gras* with plenty of truffles – out of this world! A chopped black truffle added to the sauce makes it even better!

It looked extra special because it was served on a huge silver salver, beautifully polished, surrounded by rosettes of mashed potato and decorated with sprigs of fresh parsley. Silver really does make things look good, and gives a lovely finish to almost any dish. At most of the big houses where I have worked, we used silver serving dishes every day to set the food off to its best advantage.

---

4 supremes of pheasant breast

---

4 oz (100 g) foie gras

---

pig's caul (membrane used to enclose the stuffed breasts)

¼ pint (150 ml) dry white wine

¼ pint (150 ml) water

---

2 egg yolks

¼ pint (150 ml) double cream

---

a few sprigs of parsley to garnish

---

1 teaspoon arrowroot (optional)

Flatten the supremes of pheasant slightly, then cover the tops with *foie gras* about ½ in (1 cm) thick. Wrap them in the caul and place in a sauté pan with a lid. Mix the wine and water and pour in enough to come up to the meat. Bring to the boil and poach carefully, covered, for about 20 minutes until cooked. Lift the supremes on to a serving dish, keep them warm and reserve the stock.

Bring the reserved stock to the boil and reduce to about ½ pint (300 ml). Mix together the egg yolks and cream. Remove the stock from the heat and stir 4 tablespoons of stock into the egg and cream mixture. Beat well with a whisk, then return the mixture to the pan. Re-heat gently, stirring all the time, until just boiling. Pour the sauce over the pheasant and decorate with sprigs of parsley to serve. If you feel nervous of the sauce curdling, you can add a teaspoon of arrowroot to the egg yolks.

Even though we did not speak French, we were expected to know which garnish went with each particular dish on the French menu at any of the big houses where I worked. The chef would explain it to you once, and you did not dare to ask again. He would watch you preparing it, then say, 'That's no good to me. Do it again.' We used to keep a little notebook of how to make the garnishes in case we forgot.

Pheasant with Celery Sauce

[SERVES 3 TO 4]

This recipe is good if the bird appears to be old; an old cock pheasant has spurs on the back of the leg the Horse Guards would be proud of!

As a change, you can also use cooked pheasant legs for the White Devil recipe on page 92.

4 carrots, coarsely chopped

1 onion, coarsely chopped

4 sticks celery, coarsely chopped

½ pint (300 ml) Chicken Stock (see page 198)

1 pheasant

½ pint (300 ml) Celery Sauce (see page 192)

Pre-heat the oven to 325°F (160°C), gas mark 3. Put the chopped vegetables in a large flameproof casserole dish, just cover with stock and place the pheasant on top. Bring the liquid to the boil, cover and put in the oven until the bird is cooked. This may take between 1 and 3 hours depending on the age of the bird. Remove from the casserole and carve.

Make the celery sauce and smother the pheasant meat with the sauce.

Herbed Rabbit and Onions

[SERVES 4 TO 6]

This makes a lovely lunch dish served with potatoes and a green vegetable.

1 rabbit, jointed and cut into 2 in (5 cm) pieces

2 medium onions, thinly sliced

1 tablespoon mixed herbs

salt and freshly ground black pepper

4 rashers streaky bacon

1 pint (600 ml) Chicken Stock (see page 198)

1 oz (25 g) unsalted butter, softened

1 oz (25 g) plain flour

In a large saucepan or flameproof casserole, put alternate layers of rabbit and onion, seasoning each layer with herbs, salt and freshly ground black pepper. Finish with a layer of bacon and a few slices of onion. Pour in the stock. Cover the casserole, bring to the boil and simmer gently for 2 hours or pop in the oven and cook at about 325°F (160°C), gas mark 3. Mix together the butter and flour and whisk it into the sauce a little at a time until the sauce thickens. Cook for a further 5 minutes, stirring, over a medium heat, and serve.

Jugged Hare

[SERVES 4 TO 6]

For the not too faint-hearted, it is better if the hare is skinned before paunching: this way it is easy to save the blood. Hares were always brought into the big kitchens unpaunched. They were hung by the feet so the blood drained into the chest cavity. Then you skinned them, cut through the belly, pulled out the inside and wiped it. Then if you sat them on a little basin and broke the chest membrane, all the blood drained into the basin. We mixed this with cream to help thicken the gravy (or for adding to hare soup) and to give it a delicious flavour and lovely velvety texture. I think this is something that only the older people will do, though; I have noticed these days if skinning and paunching a hare are mentioned, the nose takes an upward turn!

If the hare has kept his head and jacket on, you can tell if he's a young 'un if the ears tear easily.

FOR THE MARINADE:

½ bottle claret or good red wine

2 tablespoons salad oil

1 onion, sliced

4 juniper berries, crushed

freshly ground black pepper

1 × 6 lb (2.75 kg) hare

1 oz (25 g) unsalted butter

4 oz (100 g) streaky bacon, cut into snips

2 carrots, sliced

1 onion, sliced

4 sticks celery, sliced

1 bouquet garni

½ pint (300 ml) Chicken Stock (see page 198)

FOR THE FORCEMEAT BALLS:

1 small onion, finely chopped

1 rasher bacon, chopped

4 tablespoons fresh white breadcrumbs

1 tablespoon shredded suet

1 tablespoon chopped fresh parsley

2 teaspoons chopped fresh lemon thyme or thyme

salt and freshly ground black pepper

1 egg, beaten

1 oz (50 g) unsalted butter, softened

1 oz (50 g) plain flour

Put all the marinade ingredients in a saucepan, bring to the boil, then remove from the heat and leave to cool. Cut the hare into about 8 pieces, cover with the cold marinade, cover and leave to marinate in the fridge for about 12 hours.

Pre-heat the oven to 325°F (160°C), gas mark 3. Remove the meat from the marinade and dry it well. Melt the butter in a frying pan and fry the hare quickly until it turns a nice brown, then put it in a flameproof casserole dish. Add the bacon, carrots, onion, celery and bouquet garni. Pour in the strained marinade, and add just enough stock to cover the hare. Cover the casserole so it is as air-tight as possible and put in the oven for about 1½ hours for a young hare or up to 3 hours if the hare has seen more than two summers.

To make the forcemeat balls, mix all the ingredients together and bind with the beaten egg. If the mixture does not bind together well, add a little milk. Form the stuffing into balls and pop into the casserole about 30 minutes before the end of cooking time.

When the casserole is cooked, lift the meat, stuffing balls and vegetables on to a serving dish and bring the juices to the boil. Mix together the softened butter and flour on a plate to make a *beurre manié*, then whisk knobs of the *beurre manié* into the sauce until it thickens. Add a little more red wine or port if the casserole has become too dry. Pour the sauce over the meat and serve.

Roast Venison

[SERVES 4 TO 6]

A joint of haunch of venison is one of the best pieces for roasting. It can be quite a dry meat, so is best cooked slowly to retain the juices. This is one way we used to get the staff to eat venison before the War. If you do not like venison roast, buy some beef kidney and make it into a venison and kidney pudding.

1 × 4 lb (1.75 kg) venison joint

1 lb (450 g) plain flour

Pre-heat the oven to 375°F (190°C), gas mark 5. Mix the flour with enough water to make a thick pastry, roll it out and use it to cover the joint, making sure there are no holes in the pastry. This will cook to a thick crust. This is the older method of cooking; you can brush the joint with oil or butter and wrap it in foil before cooking, if you prefer. Place the joint in a roasting tin and roast in the oven for about 35 minutes per 1 lb (450 g). About 20 minutes before the end of cooking time, remove the pastry or foil to allow the joint to brown. Serve with redcurrant jelly, mashed potato and a green vegetable.

Part Six

VEGETABLES AND SALADS

Savoury Stuffed Peppers

[SERVES 4]

You can vary this recipe depending on what you have in the fridge. Oddments of ham can be used instead of the bacon, or a few chopped chicken livers, cooked chicken or white fish can be substituted for the mince. Stuffed peppers are nice served with Quick Tomato Sauce (see page 66).

---

4 green or red peppers

---

4 oz (100 g) white or brown long-grain rice

---

1 oz (25 g) unsalted butter

---

1 small onion, chopped

---

2 oz (50 g) mushrooms, chopped

---

2 rashers lean bacon, finely chopped

---

6 oz (175 g) minced beef

---

a pinch of oregano

---

salt and freshly ground black pepper

---

1 small egg, lightly beaten

---

4 oz (100 g) Cheddar cheese, grated

Pre-heat the oven to 350°F (180°C), gas mark 4. Slice the peppers in half lengthways and remove the seeds and membrane. Put the peppers in a basin and cover with boiling water. Leave to stand for about 5 minutes, then remove them and turn them upside down to drain. Simmer the rice in boiling salted water for about 10 minutes or until tender, then drain. Melt the butter in a frying pan and gently fry the onion, mushrooms and bacon for 5 minutes. Add the mince and cook for about 10 minutes, stirring well, until the mince is cooked through. Mix in the rice and season with oregano and salt and freshly ground black pepper. Remove the pan from the heat and stir in the lightly beaten egg. Arrange the peppers in a buttered ovenproof dish, spoon the mixture into the peppers and cover them with the grated cheese. Pour 2 tablespoons of water into the dish and put it in the oven for 35 to 40 minutes until the peppers are soft and the cheese golden brown.

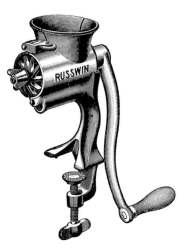

Braised Celery Hearts

[SERVES 4]

This is a lazy way of braising celery, but it is very appetising – tasty and nice and brown-looking. Keep a tin of celery hearts and a tin of beef consommé in your store cupboard and the recipe is easy to do at any time. You can use fresh celery hearts, of course, but you would need to cut them in half and simmer them in stock until tender before following the recipe.

---

1 × 15 oz (425 g) tin celery hearts

2 oz (50 g) unsalted butter

1 × 15 oz (425 g) tin beef consommé

Pre-heat the oven to 350°F (180°C), gas mark 4. Drain the celery well on kitchen paper. Melt the butter in a frying pan and fry the celery until browned. Put the celery in a flameproof casserole dish and pour in the consommé. Bring to the boil, cover and put in the oven for about 15 minutes until heated through. Remove the celery to a serving dish, bring the consommé to the boil and reduce it to a rich glaze. Pour the glaze over the celery and serve.

Savoy Cabbage with Bacon and Onion

[SERVES 4]

---

1 lb (450 g) Savoy cabbage, coarsely shredded

1 oz (25 g) unsalted butter

1 onion, chopped

4 oz (100 g) bacon, rind removed and chopped

salt and freshly ground black pepper

a pinch of nutmeg

Cook the cabbage in boiling salted water for about 6 minutes until just cooked, then drain it and press out all the liquid. Melt the butter in a saucepan and fry the onion for about 3 minutes until soft but not browned. Add the bacon and fry for a further 3 minutes. Mix in the cabbage, season well with salt and freshly ground black pepper and serve sprinkled with nutmeg.

I usually cook for six or eight of the family on a Sunday and we always have meat, although I don't eat as much during the week. When you get older you tend not to eat so much meat, but loads of vegetables instead. It was really lovely when we were at The Victorian Kitchen *gardens and Harry brought in all the vegetables fresh from the soil.*

Creamy Stuffed Marrow Rings

[SERVES 4]

The simple taste of marrow goes well with a stuffing, and you can use up odds and ends for the stuffing if you wish, such as the remains of a joint or chicken. If you have a small marrow, just peel it and scoop out the seeds with a spoon, blanch it for 3 to 5 minutes, then fill the cavity and put the top back on with a cocktail stick before baking.

---

1 marrow, peeled, deseeded and cut into 3 in (7.5 cm) deep rings

---

8 oz (225 g) minced beef

---

1 tablespoon chopped fresh parsley

---

salt and freshly ground black pepper

½ pint (300 ml) Béchamel Sauce (see page 194)

Pre-heat the oven to 350°F (180°C), gas mark 4. Put the marrow rings in a saucepan of lightly salted water, bring to the boil and simmer for about 5 minutes, then drain them well. Place them in a buttered roasting tin. Mix the mince and parsley and season it well with salt and freshly ground black pepper. Stir in the béchamel sauce, and spoon the mixture into the marrow rings. Cover with buttered greaseproof paper and bake for about 20 minutes until the marrow is soft.

Duchesse Potato Rounds

[SERVES 4]

Duchesse potatoes are so versatile, you can do almost anything with them, so it is often a good idea to prepare a larger quantity than you need and freeze some ready for another occasion.

---

1 lb (450 g) potatoes

---

1 oz (25 g) unsalted butter

---

salt and freshly ground black pepper

---

1 egg yolk

---

beaten egg to glaze

Cook the potatoes in boiling salted water until tender. Drain them well, then mash them with the butter and season to taste with salt and freshly ground black pepper. Over a gentle heat, mix in the egg yolk and beat until the mixture is smooth. Pre-heat the oven to 400°F (200°C), gas mark 6. Shape spoonfuls of the mixture into small rounds and put them on a greased baking tray. Mark a lattice pattern on the top with the blunt side of a knife and brush with beaten egg. Bake them in the oven for about 20 minutes until golden.

Another way to bake Duchesse Potatoes is to put the mixture into a piping bag with a star nozzle and pipe rosettes on to the greased baking tray, and bake as above.

You can also make the mixture into croquettes by shaping it into rolls and dipping them in egg and breadcrumbs before frying in shallow oil and butter.

OPPOSITE] *Gallantine (page 96).*

OVERLEAF] *Sara's Meat Roll (page 67); Autumn Vegetable Casserole (page 127).*

Chicken Broccoli Surprise (page 93).

OPPOSITE] *Brandy and Tarragon Poussins (page 98).*
OVERLEAF] *Crispy Cauliflower Cake (page 122); Mushrooms with Chicken Liver Stuffing (page 125).*

Lamb-Roast Potato and Onion

Illustrated on page 74
[SERVES 4]

This is a really easy way to cook vegetables to go with your Sunday roast. It is important not to wash the potatoes after you have peeled and sliced them as the starch in the potatoes helps to mould the potatoes and onions together.

---

1 lb (450 g) potatoes, peeled and sliced

---

4 onions, sliced

---

salt and freshly ground black pepper

Layer the potatoes and onions in the bottom of a well-buttered roasting tin. Season to taste with salt and freshly ground black pepper. Place a grid on top on which to roast your lamb joint. Roast as usual at 350°F (180°C), gas mark 4. The fat from the meat will drip through to flavour and help cook the vegetables.

I love to eat the skins of jacket potatoes. When you have eaten the insides, cut a long strip of fresh butter and roll the skin round it. You'll be surprised how tasty it is!

Buttered Crumb Cauliflower

[SERVES 4]

Cauliflower always seems to make an entrance either plain boiled with a scattering of parsley or 'au gratin', although I think it is nicer simply fried in butter with a squeeze of lemon juice. Try this different way of serving it, but remember to fry the crumbs in butter otherwise they will not be nice and crunchy.

---

1 cauliflower, separated into florets

---

4 oz (100 g) unsalted butter

---

2 tablespoons fresh white breadcrumbs

---

2 hard-boiled eggs, chopped

---

2 tablespoons chopped fresh parsley or chives

Put the florets in a saucepan of lightly salted water, bring to the boil and simmer for about 5 minutes until just tender, then drain well. Heat the butter in a large frying pan until sizzling and turn the florets into the butter. Coat them in butter but do not allow them to get too brown. Lift them on to a serving dish. Add the crumbs to the pan and fry them until they are crisp and brown. Mix in the hard-boiled eggs and 1 tablespoon parsley or chives and spoon this over the cauliflower. Sprinkle with the remaining parsley or chives.

Crispy Cauliflower Cake

Illustrated on page 118

[SERVES 4]

If you have a cauliflower in the garden that has 'blown', or you have bought one that is not very white, try making this cake. You will need a little more cauliflower per person than usual. This dish goes well with roast lamb.

1 large cauliflower, separated into florets
4 oz (100 g) unsalted butter
8 oz (225 g) fresh brown breadcrumbs
salt and freshly ground black pepper

Pre-heat the oven to 375°F (190°C), gas mark 5. Put the florets in a saucepan of lightly salted water, bring to the boil and simmer for about 5 minutes until just tender, then drain well. Melt the butter in a frying pan, mix in the breadcrumbs and fry until golden brown. Well butter a 2 pint (1.2 litre) soufflé dish and coat all over with crumbs. Put in a layer of cauliflower then a layer of crumbs alternately to the top of the dish, seasoning as you go, and finishing with a layer of crumbs. Press the crumbs well in between the cauliflower otherwise the 'cake' will turn out a pancake! Put in the oven for about 15 minutes to re-heat, then turn out on to a serving plate.

Tangy Tomato Cauliflower

[SERVES 4]

This tangy, creamy sauce makes cauliflower into quite an exciting side dish which you could serve with pork chops or a fillet of white fish.

1 cauliflower
2 oz (50 g) unsalted butter
3 shallots, chopped
2 tablespoons white wine vinegar
¼ pint (150 ml) double cream
2 tablespoons tomato ketchup
salt and freshly ground black pepper
1 tablespoon chopped fresh parsley or chives

Cut a cross in the stalk of the cauliflower and put it in a large saucepan of lightly salted water. Bring to the boil and simmer for about 15 minutes until cooked, then drain and transfer to a serving dish. Meanwhile, melt the butter in a frying pan and fry the shallots until soft but not browned. Add the wine vinegar and boil to reduce the liquid a little. Allow it to cool, then work in the cream and tomato ketchup and season to taste with salt and freshly ground black pepper. Re-heat, but do not allow the sauce to boil. Pour the sauce over the cauliflower and scatter the parsley or chives over the top to give it a little colour.

Brussels Sprouts with Chestnuts

[SERVES 4]

Most people like this dish at Christmas as it goes well with turkey. You can either take the children to find the chestnuts at half term, or buy the imported ones. I usually use the imported ones, although it's a swings and roundabouts game. The English ones are small and often wither, but the imported ones have a good proportion of black inside. Anyway, don't let this stop you as the chestnuts can be prepared beforehand and will freeze.

---

1 lb (450 g) chestnuts

---

1 pint (600 ml) turkey stock (made as Chicken Stock, see page 198)

---

2 lb (1 kg) Brussels sprouts

---

3 oz (75 g) unsalted butter

---

freshly ground black pepper

Pre-heat the oven to 350°F (180°C), gas mark 4. Cut a nick in the skin of the chestnuts and put them in a large saucepan of cold water. Bring to the boil, then take the pan off the heat and peel off the shell and skin together. When they get a bit difficult to skin, return the pan to the heat and bring up to the boil again. Put the chestnuts in a casserole dish with the turkey stock and put in the oven for about 30 minutes until tender. Meanwhile, put the sprouts in a saucepan of lightly salted water, bring to the boil and simmer for about 10 minutes until they are cooked but still slightly crunchy, then drain them well. Heat the butter in a frying pan until it is foaming, then add the sprouts and chestnuts, turning until the sprouts just begin to go a crunchy brown. Season with freshly ground black pepper and turn into a serving dish.

Last Christmas, I bought some of the loveliest-looking sprouts I have seen for many years – fresh, crisp and green. But they were so bitter when they were cooked that we could hardly eat them. I wonder if the changing flavours of our vegetables have a lot to do with what we are putting on the soil. We have soured it with fertilisers and pesticides and now we are reaping the consequences. We never used to have potatoes which boiled to a floury mush. Perhaps more farmers should go back to the old traditional farming methods.

Herb-Cream Courgettes

[SERVES 4]

I like courgettes cooked this way, whether you slice larger ones into rounds or use the tiny ones whole, but do not overcook them. It is far better to have a slight bite to them than a soggy mess. You can replace the parsley and basil with tarragon or rosemary, but remember rosemary is a very strong herb so too little is better than too much.

---

1 lb (450 g) courgettes

---

1 oz (25 g) unsalted butter

---

3 tablespoons double cream, yoghurt or fromage frais

---

salt and freshly ground black pepper

---

1 tablespoon chopped fresh parsley

½ tablespoon chopped fresh basil

---

a sprig of parsley to garnish

If you can find courgettes about as big as your little finger, boil them in lightly salted water for 4 to 5 minutes until they just begin to lose their firmness, then drain them. For fuller grown courgettes, slice them into ½ in (1 cm) rounds and blanch them in lightly salted boiling water for 1 minute, then drain. Melt the butter in a saucepan and add the remaining ingredients. Add the drained courgettes and shake over the heat until the courgettes are coated in the herb cream. Do not allow the mixture to boil, especially if you are using yoghurt or fromage frais as they tend to separate. Turn on to a serving dish and decorate with a sprig of parsley.

We were never allowed to eat snacks outside the house as children. We had our meals at home and that was it. And we couldn't have any pudding unless we ate our meat and vegetables! Mother only put a bit on the side of the plate of something we didn't like, such as parsnips or swede, but we had to eat it and eventually grew to like it. There were plenty of vegetables we did like, such as cauliflower, and as Dad was a keen gardener we always had masses of vegetables at home.

Mushrooms with Chicken Liver Stuffing

Illustrated on page 119

[SERVES 4]

Choose large mushrooms for this dish with a good lip to them so that they hold the stuffing. You can use a piece of lamb's liver if you prefer, but the chicken livers give a nice delicate taste.

---

8 oz (225 g) large mushrooms

2 shallots, chopped

2 rashers bacon, chopped

1 oz (25 g) unsalted butter

8 oz (225 g) chicken livers, finely chopped

1 tablespoon chopped fresh parsley

salt and freshly ground black pepper

4 oz (100 g) fresh white breadcrumbs

4 oz (100 g) Cheddar cheese, grated

Pre-heat the oven to 400°F (200°C), gas mark 6. Wipe the mushrooms but don't skin them. Take off the stems and chop them, then mix them with the shallots and bacon. Melt the butter in a frying pan and fry the mushroom stalks, shallots and bacon for about 2 minutes, then add the chicken livers and parsley, season to taste with salt and freshly ground black pepper and continue to fry for about 5 minutes until cooked through. Add enough of the breadcrumbs to make a nice soft mixture and use this to fill the mushroom caps. Place them in a buttered roasting tin, cover with foil and put in the oven for 15 to 20 minutes. Remove the foil, sprinkle on the cheese and return them to the oven or pop them under the grill for a few minutes until the cheese melts.

Braised Onions with Cheese Sauce

[SERVES 4]

This recipe can be served with or without the cheese sauce as a tasty snack or a vegetable. It goes particularly well with roast meats.

1 lb (450 g) small or medium-sized onions
1 oz (25 g) unsalted butter
½ pint (300 ml) beef stock
½ pint (300 ml) Cheese Sauce (see page 192)

Pre-heat the oven to 350°F (180°C), gas mark 4. Select onions which are about the same size. Remove the skins, carefully trim the root end so the onions will not fall apart and cut high on the stem end. Melt the butter in a flameproof casserole and fry the onions for about 6 minutes until browned all over. Add the stock, cover the casserole and cook in the oven for about 40 minutes until nice and brown. Serve with the cheese sauce.

Crunchy Cheese Celeriac

[SERVES 4]

Celeriac can be bought at most supermarkets. It is not a very elegant root vegetable, but can be useful in the kitchen. It makes a lovely addition to soups, can be grated and used in salads, is tasty with dips, and is nice as a vegetable, peeled and used like turnip or swede. Always use it as soon as it has been peeled, or put it into lemon or vinegar water to prevent it from going brown.

1 lb (450 g) celeriac, cut into ½ in (1 cm) slices
½ pint (300 ml) Cheese Sauce (see page 192)
2 tomatoes, sliced
salt and freshly ground black pepper
2 oz (50 g) fresh white breadcrumbs
2 oz (50 g) Cheddar cheese, grated
1 oz (25 g) unsalted butter

Put the celeriac in a saucepan of lightly salted water, bring to the boil and simmer for about 20 minutes until tender. Drain well and place in a gratin dish. Pour over the cheese sauce and lay the sliced tomatoes on top. Season to taste with salt and freshly ground black pepper. Mix the breadcrumbs and grated cheese and sprinkle them over the dish, then dot a few knobs of butter on top. Place under a hot grill for about 5 minutes until brown and bubbling.

Autumn Vegetable Casserole

Illustrated on page 115

[SERVES 4]

This is a lovely tasty casserole which makes use of any nice fresh vegetables you have available, a little stock (make sure you don't drown it) and lots of black pepper. It cooks best in an earthenware casserole with a lid; I bought mine in a jumble sale ages ago! My sister used to make this casserole on a Saturday during the War when the boys were playing football in the afternoon. Once it was all prepared and in the oven, they could come in and help themselves whenever they liked.

---

4 tablespoons oil

---

2 lb (1 kg) mixed vegetables (onions, carrots, turnips, swedes, parsnips, etc.), coarsely chopped

---

2 tablespoons plain flour

½ pint (300 ml) vegetable or Chicken Stock (see page 198)

---

salt and freshly ground black pepper

---

a squeeze of lemon juice

---

a sprig of fresh thyme

---

grated Cheddar cheese to serve

Pre-heat the oven to 325°F (160°C), gas mark 3. Heat the oil in a frying pan and fry the vegetables in batches until browned, then pop them into the casserole. Mix in the flour and stock; but don't drown the vegetables as they will create their own juice as they cook. Season well with salt and freshly ground black pepper and a squeeze of lemon juice, add the thyme and cook in a moderate oven for about 2 hours, stirring occasionally. Serve with grated Cheddar cheese.

VEGETABLE IDEAS

I like lots of plain vegetables – steamed or boiled with a knob of butter. But here are a few more ideas for you to try.

Carrots can be used all the year round – in salads, soups and casseroles. Young ones are something special, and I think they are best just plain boiled with a pinch of sugar and dished up slightly firm or covered with chopped fresh parsley, chives or mint – and needless to say, don't forget the large knob of butter! Older carrots can be boiled, then mixed with peas and stirred into a Béchamel Sauce (see page 194) flavoured with your favourite herb.

Fennel has an aniseed taste. Raw fennel goes well in salads, or you could have it cooked, with fish. Quarter or halve the bulbs and simmer them until just tender. Then drain them well and fry them in foaming butter until brown on all sides.

Marrow is one of my favourite vegetables. Sometimes I just have rings of marrow with a little melted butter, salt and lots of freshly ground black pepper for a light lunch. Chunks of boiled, drained marrow are good tossed in melted butter and grated strong cheese and then fried for a few minutes until golden brown.

Parsnips are tasty roasted, or I boil them until tender and wring them out in a cloth before mashing them and re-heating them with a good knob of butter and plenty of salt and freshly ground black pepper. They perk up bubble and squeak, too.

Swede and turnip are much the same; they seem to be accepted in casseroles and soups but get the thumbs-down treatment as a vegetable! You can cook swede in the same way as parsnips. Try baby turnips as a garnish round roast lamb, with a Navarin of Lamb (see page 70), serve them with peas or toss them in butter and chopped parsley.

Season boiled or steamed spinach with salt, black pepper and a little nutmeg to bring out the taste, then purée it with a spoonful of cream or melted butter. This is an easy recipe to make in a fairly large quantity, then freeze in small batches to take out and re-heat when you need it.

Salmagundi

[SERVES 6 TO 8]

The appeal of this recipe lies in the presentation and you can choose the amounts and ingredients to suit your own requirements. When we made the dish in *The Victorian Kitchen* television series, I put a few anchovies across the top in a sort of star-fish pattern which makes a very attractive decoration.

---

4 hard-boiled eggs, yolks and whites, finely chopped separately

---

4 oz (100 g) cooked chicken or veal, finely chopped

---

4 oz (100 g) fresh beetroot, boiled, finely chopped and seasoned with 1 tablespoon vinegar and freshly ground black pepper

---

4 oz (100 g) pickled red cabbage, finely chopped

---

4 oz (100 g) lean ham, finely chopped

---

2 oz (50 g) tongue, finely chopped

---

1 × 4 oz (100 g) tin anchovies, drained

---

a bunch of parsley to garnish

Turn a deep saucer or a wide teacup upside down on a serving plate. Arrange the ingredients in circles around the plate and over the saucer, making the rows at the bottom wider than the top ones, narrowing them gradually and varying the colours as much as possible and contrasting them nicely. Arrange a sprig of curled parsley on top and garnish with a border of parsley.

Apple, Walnut and Sultana Salad

[SERVES 4]

I often put together salads with whatever I have in the fridge, but it always pays to try something different from time to time, and don't be afraid not to use the traditional salad ingredients – lettuce, tomatoes and so on – all the time. You can try out the variety of lettuces now available in the supermarkets, and add a little red lettuce for colour. If you do not wish to make your own mayonnaise, there are plenty of excellent brands on the market.

---

2 oz (50 g) sultanas

---

2 oz (50 g) walnuts with skin

---

3 dessert apples, cored and cut into half moon shapes

¼ pint (150 ml) Creamy Mayonnaise (see page 197)

---

lettuce

Soak the sultanas in boiling water for about 15 minutes, then drain. Chop the walnuts coarsely. Mix the walnuts, sultanas and apples together and coat in the mayonnaise. Serve on a bed of lettuce leaves.

Coleslaw with Walnuts and Celery

[SERVES 6 TO 8]

I never measure the ingredients for my coleslaw; you get to know the right quantities after a while. I use a knife to shred the cabbage, but a grater is better for the carrots as they do not seem to be so wet. Coleslaw is best eaten as soon as it is made so that it is nice and crunchy; I can't bear wet coleslaw. If I want to make the salad for the next day, I leave out the grated carrot and mix the other ingredients with the carrot and dressing when I am ready. I have had the dressing recipe for such a long time that I cannot remember where it came from. You can make it up in advance without the cream and keep it in a jar in the fridge for about 2 weeks. Make sure you beat in the egg while the mixture is still hot.

1 lb (450 g) white cabbage, finely shredded

4 carrots, grated

4 spring onions, finely chopped

2 sticks celery, finely chopped

2 oz (50 g) walnuts, finely chopped

FOR THE COLESLAW DRESSING:

2 oz (50 g) caster sugar

1 oz (50 g) plain flour

1 teaspoon salt

1 tablespoon made mustard

¼ pint (150 ml) white vinegar, white wine vinegar or tarragon vinegar

¼ pint (150 ml) water

1 egg, beaten

1 oz (25 g) unsalted butter

2 tablespoons single cream, yoghurt or fromage frais

Mix all the coleslaw ingredients together.

To make the dressing, mix the sugar, flour and salt to a paste with a little water. Add the mustard. Bring the vinegar and water to the boil in a saucepan and pour on to the mixed ingredients, beating well. Return the mixture to the pan, bring back to the boil and simmer for about 5 minutes. Remove from the heat and beat in the egg and butter. Allow to cool. When cold, cover and store in the fridge until needed, then thin down with cream, yoghurt or fromage frais and mix into the coleslaw.

Crunchy Mixed Pepper Rice Salad

[SERVES 4 TO 6]

For a simple pepper salad, just slice the three coloured peppers into rings and coat in French Dressing (see page 196). It tastes lovely and the colours are wonderful. This recipe is very adaptable, so try it like this and then vary it according to what you have in the store cupboard.

---

1 red pepper, deseeded and cut into squares

---

1 green pepper, deseeded and cut into squares

---

1 yellow pepper, deseeded and cut into squares

---

2 oz (50 g) cooked long-grain rice

---

4 spring onions, sliced
or 1 tablespoon chopped fresh chives

---

1 oz (25 g) pine kernels

$\frac{1}{4}$ pint (150 ml) French Dressing (see page 196)

---

2 spring onions to garnish

Mix together all the ingredients except the spring onion for the garnish and stir in the French dressing. To make the garnish, finely slice the spring onions lengthways, keeping about 1 in (2.5 cm) of the white end intact, and leave them in ice cold water for about 15 minutes to curl up. Garnish the salad with the spring onions.

If you keep a few tins of beans in the store cupboard, you can put a tasty salad together in no time. Any combination of beans can be used, but I like red kidney beans, flageolet beans and haricot beans as the colours look especially nice. Wash and drain them well, then pile them in a salad bowl, surround them with a few lettuce leaves or watercress and pour on some French Dressing (see page 196).

Part Seven

DESSERTS

Demerara-Rum Apple Pudding

[SERVES 4 TO 6]

This delicious pudding has a lovely brown crust and makes lots of tasty juice. It is delicious served with cream or custard. You can cover and tie it down with kitchen foil, but I prefer the old cloth – it's age you see!

---

8 oz (225 g) plain flour

4 oz (100 g) shredded suet

2 tablespoons water

4 oz (100 g) demerara sugar

4 oz (100 g) unsalted butter

2 tablespoons rum

2 lb (1 kg) cooking apples, peeled, cored, quartered and thinly sliced

6 cloves

Mix the flour and suet and stir in just enough water to bind together the mixture to a pastry. Well butter a 2 pint (1.2 litre) pudding basin. Put in a spoonful of the demerara sugar and roll it all round until the basin is well coated. Use about two-thirds of the pastry to line the basin, reserving enough for the top. Mix the butter, remaining sugar and the rum on a plate and make it into little balls about the size of a penny. Put a thick layer of apple slices into the pastry, then add a few sugar balls and a clove. Continue layering in this way until you have filled it to the top. Moisten the edge of the pastry and stick on the crust, sealing the edges well. Cover with greaseproof paper and a pudding cloth and tie it round with string. Place the basin in a large saucepan and fill it with water to come halfway up the basin. Bring to the boil and steam for about $2\frac{1}{2}$ hours, topping up with boiling water as necessary. Turn the pudding out on to a dish with a deep rim, as it makes a lot of juice. Serve with cream or custard.

Layered Syrup Pudding

[SERVES 4]

Steamed suet puddings were always popular in the large houses, and this special syrup pudding was a particular favourite.

8 oz (225 g) self-raising flour
a pinch of salt
4 oz (100 g) shredded suet
$\frac{1}{4}$ pint (150 ml) water
5 tablespoons golden syrup

Sift the flour and salt into a basin, add the suet and stir in enough water to make a light dough. Warm the syrup slightly. I stand the tin on the storage heater in winter, but you can stand it in a saucepan of hot water. Put a spoonful of syrup in the bottom of a well buttered 2 pint (1.2 litre) pudding basin. Roll out the pastry and cut a circle to fit the bottom of the basin. Spoon a tablespoonful of syrup over the pastry, then lay in another round of pastry. Continue layering syrup and pastry until you have about 6 pastry layers sandwiched with syrup, ending with pastry on the top. Cover with greaseproof paper and a pudding cloth secured with string. Place the pudding basin in a large saucepan filled with water to come halfway up the basin. Bring the water to the boil and steam the pudding for 3 hours, topping up with boiling water as necessary.

Treacle Pudding

[SERVES 4 TO 6]

This recipe is about 100 years old. It's a lovely, dark-coloured pudding, very light in texture, and would make a good alternative to Christmas pudding.

4 oz (100 g) currants
4 oz (100 g) shredded suet
4 oz (100 g) fresh white breadcrumbs
4 oz (100 g) self-raising flour
1 tablespoon sugar
$\frac{1}{2}$ teaspoon salt
1 teaspoon ground ginger
$\frac{1}{2}$ teaspoon bicarbonate of soda
$\frac{1}{4}$ teaspoon cream of tartar
8 oz (225 g) treacle
1 egg, beaten
8 fl oz (250 ml) water

Mix all the dry ingredients together, then stir in the treacle. Combine the egg and water, and mix them into the other ingredients until the mixture is moist but not sloppy, adding a little extra water if needed. Turn the mixture into a greased 2 pint (1.2 litre) pudding basin and cover with greased greaseproof paper and a pudding cloth secured with string. Place in a saucepan filled with water to come halfway up the basin, bring the water to the boil, cover the saucepan and steam for 1$\frac{1}{2}$ hours, topping up with boiling water as necessary.

Guards' Pudding

[SERVES 4]

This is a very easy pudding to make for a family lunch – it's nice and light and not too sweet.

---

6 oz (175 g) fresh white breadcrumbs

4 oz (100 g) light soft brown sugar

1 teaspoon bicarbonate of soda

4 oz (100 g) butter, melted

2 eggs, well beaten

3 tablespoons strawberry jam

Mix together the dry ingredients, stir in the melted butter, then the eggs and jam. Turn into a well buttered 2 pint (1.2 litre) pudding basin, cover with greaseproof paper and a pudding cloth secured with string and place the basin in a large saucepan filled with water to come halfway up the basin. Bring to the boil and steam for 1½ hours, keeping the water on the boil. Top up with boiling water as necessary. Serve with strawberry jam and cream.

Toffee Pudding

Illustrated on page 153

[SERVES 4]

This is another children's pudding which sounds unusual but is very nice and is a good way of using up any stale bread. It is best if you make a good pile of the fried bread and serve with plenty of cream.

---

8 oz (225 g) stale bread, sliced 1 in (2.5 cm) thick, crusts removed and cut in half

¼ pint (150 ml) milk

2 oz (50 g) demerara sugar

2 oz (50 g) unsalted butter

4 oz (100 g) golden syrup

½ pint (300 ml) double or whipping cream, lightly whipped

Dip the prepared slices of bread quickly in the milk on both sides. Bring the sugar, butter and syrup to the boil in a frying pan and simmer until light brown in colour. Fry the bread lightly in the mixture and then pile it on to a hot dish and serve with the whipped cream.

Bibury Pudding

[SERVES 4 TO 6]

We once went on a family visit to a trout farm in Bibury in the Cotswolds. It is a lovely day out for the children because they can see all the stages of the fishes' development, and you can buy a bag of food to feed the fish. By chance we went for lunch to a little pub nearby called The Catherine Wheel. The food we had was beautifully cooked, and I talked to the owner about his cooking. He said his bread pudding was different from everyone else's, so we decided to try it. When it came, it was the most colossal portion we had ever seen – and it was delicious. My mother used to make a nice bread pudding, but it was nothing to this. It is wonderful hot or cold, but don't be tempted to leave out the alcohol; that is what makes it special.

$\frac{1}{2}$ large sliced loaf
1 pint (600 ml) boiling water
4 oz (100 g) lard, boiling
$1\frac{1}{2}$ lb (750 g) dried mixed fruit
4 oz (100 g) caster sugar
1 egg, beaten
$2\frac{1}{2}$ fl oz (65 ml) port
$2\frac{1}{2}$ fl oz (65 ml) brandy

Put the bread in a large bowl and pour on the boiling water. Put a towel over the top to keep in the heat and leave it to soak for about 2 hours.

Pre-heat the oven to 350°F (180°C), gas mark 4. The bread should be soggy but not too wet, so drain off any excess water. Mash the bread with a potato masher, then add the boiling lard and mix in all the remaining ingredients. Turn into a greased 8 in (20 cm) square tin and bake for about $1\frac{1}{2}$ hours until the dried fruit begins to go black on the top. If the top gets very brown before the pudding is cooked, turn down the oven a bit. Serve with double cream or ice-cream.

If you are whisking or beating small quantities of egg or cream, just put one blade into the electric hand whisk and put the egg or cream in a measuring jug.

Rum-Baked Bananas with Jam

[SERVES 4]

This is an easy dessert which everyone will love. You can substitute yoghurt or fromage frais for the cream if you prefer.

4 ripe bananas, peeled

3 tablespoons apricot jam

a squeeze of lemon juice

3 tablespoons whisky or rum

½ pint (300 ml) double or whipping cream, lightly whipped

Pre-heat the oven to 350°F (180°C), gas mark 4. Make 4 pieces of kitchen foil into boat shapes and put them into a roasting tin. Place a banana in each piece of foil and spoon over the jam, lemon juice and whisky or rum. Pull up the foil to cover the top, then bake in the oven for about 10 minutes, but do not allow the bananas to become too soft. Serve on to individual plates in the foil and let each person unwrap their own banana. Serve with the whipped cream.

Gainsborough Tart

[SERVES 4]

I hate pies with soggy bottoms, so I always heat up my baking sheet first before I make the pie. That way, the pastry begins to cook straight away and you get a nice browned bottom! I don't know what will happen to this book, because I do such naughty things in the kitchen, but they do work!

8 oz (225 g) Shortcrust Pastry (see page 199)

1 oz (25 g) unsalted butter

½ teaspoon baking powder

2 oz (50 g) caster sugar

4 oz (100 g) desiccated coconut

2 eggs, beaten

2 oz (50 g) glacé cherries, chopped, or 3 tablespoons cherry or strawberry jam

Pre-heat the oven to 350°F (180°C), gas mark 4, and heat a baking sheet in the oven. Prepare the pastry and roll it out. In a separate bowl, let the butter soften, then beat in the baking powder, sugar, coconut and eggs. The mixture should be soft but not runny. If it is too stiff, mix in a little milk. Use the pastry to line an 8 in (20 cm) flan tin or pie dish. Spread the bottom with the glacé cherries or jam and spread over the filling mixture. Place the flan dish on the hot baking sheet and bake for about 30 minutes until golden brown.

Bakewell Tart

[SERVES 4]

This is a recipe I found in a paper years ago. It's different, though not cheap to make. As I like the flavour of almond, I add the extra almond essence, but do be careful not to use too much.

8 oz (225 g) Shortcrust Pastry (see page 199)

4 tablespoons raspberry jam

4 eggs, beaten

8 oz (225 g) caster sugar

8 oz (225 g) unsalted butter, just melted

4 oz (100 g) ground almonds

3–4 drops almond essence (optional)

Pre-heat the oven to 400°F (200°C), gas mark 6 and heat a baking sheet in the oven. Make the pastry and use it to line a greased 8 in (20 cm) flan ring. Spread the bottom with raspberry jam. Beat the eggs and sugar together until pale and runny, then slowly add the melted butter and finally the ground almonds, and almond essence, if using. Pour the mixture into the pastry case, stand the flan ring on the hot baking sheet and bake for about 30 minutes until set.

Baked Lemon Pudding

[SERVES 4]

This is a two-way pudding: sponge on top and a kind of baked custard underneath.

grated rind and juice of 1 large or 2 small lemons

2 oz (50 g) unsalted butter, softened

3 oz (75 g) caster sugar

2 eggs, separated

2 tablespoons self-raising flour

8 fl oz (250 ml) milk, lukewarm

Pre-heat the oven to 350°F (180°C), gas mark 4. Beat the lemon rind into the butter with a wooden spoon. Then beat in the sugar until light and fluffy. Stir in the lemon juice, egg yolks and flour, then stir in the lukewarm milk. Whisk the egg whites until they form soft peaks and carefully fold them into the mixture. Turn the mixture into a greased pie dish and place it in a roasting tin. Pour in enough boiling water to come halfway up the sides of the pie dish. Bake for 30 to 35 minutes until golden brown and firm to touch. Serve at once.

Queen's Pudding

[SERVES 4]

In the old days, all the women had to be good cooks, although I remember Billy Giddings, a widower who lived across the road from us, coming to tell my mother he was getting married again.

'She ain't much of a 'and at pastry-making,' he told my mother, 'but 'er can flobber up a puddun!'

Whether she cooked this one or not, I wouldn't know, but it is a lovely old-fashioned pudding.

---

rind of 1 lemon, thinly peeled

½ pint (300 ml) milk

½ oz (15 g) unsalted butter

---

5 oz (150 g) caster sugar

---

2 oz (50 g) fresh white breadcrumbs

---

2 eggs, separated

---

4 tablespoons raspberry or strawberry jam

Pre-heat the oven to 350°F (180°C), gas mark 4. Place the lemon rind and milk in a saucepan, bring to the boil, cover, remove from the heat and leave for 10 minutes to infuse. Strain the milk over the butter, 1 oz (25 g) of the sugar and the breadcrumbs. Mix together and leave to cool. Mix in the egg yolks. Grease a pie dish and spread with most of the jam. Turn the mixture into the dish and leave to stand for 30 minutes, then bake for 30 to 40 minutes until set. Remove the pudding from the oven and leave to cool a little, then spread the remaining jam on top. Whip the egg whites until firm and fold in the remaining sugar. Spread this on top of the pudding. Sprinkle the top with caster sugar and return to the oven at 300°F (150°C), gas mark 2 for about 15 minutes until crisp and light brown. Serve with cream.

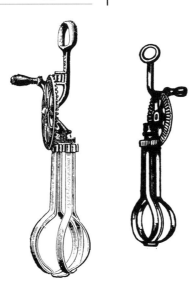

Coffee and Walnut Gâteau

Illustrated on page 155

[SERVES 4]

This is a lovely dessert for a party, especially as it can all be prepared in advance. Make sure you trim the ends of the biscuits and brush the tin with melted butter before you start to assemble the gâteau, otherwise the biscuits keep falling down and tempers tend to fray!

---

6 oz (175 g) unsalted butter

---

3 oz (75 g) icing sugar

---

1 tablespoon very strong black coffee or a few drops of coffee essence to taste

---

3 egg yolks

---

2 oz (50 g) walnuts, chopped

---

4 fl oz (120 ml) strong black coffee, cold

2–3 tablespoons Tia Maria

---

2 tablespoons melted butter

---

24 boudoir biscuits

¼ pint (150 ml) double or whipping cream, whipped

---

2 oz (50 g) walnut halves

Cream the butter and icing sugar until pale and fluffy. Gradually beat in the strong black coffee or coffee essence and egg yolks, then stir in the chopped walnuts. Mix together the coffee and Tia Maria in a shallow container. Brush a 7 in (18 cm) cake tin with melted butter. Trim the ends of 15 boudoir biscuits, dip them quickly in the coffee liquid and stand them up around the sides of the cake tin. Dip 3 more biscuits and layer them in the base of the tin. Pour in half the creamed mixture, then a layer of dipped biscuits, the remaining mixture and finally a layer of dipped biscuits. Trim the tops of the biscuits round the edge and add the bits to the top layer. Cover with kitchen foil and chill in the fridge for 24 hours before turning out on to a serving plate and decorating with swirls of whipped cream and walnut halves.

I was dreadful at hearth stoning the hearth. One day I was brought back from my half day to do it again. I had changed out of my uniform and dark stockings into light stockings. I quickly changed back into my working clothes but left the stockings because I was tearing to get out. But I was sent back because I hadn't the right stockings! You soon learnt to do things right the first time when your precious half day was at stake.

Lemon Custard Mould

[SERVES 4]

This is one of the recipes that we filmed for *The Victorian Kitchen* series, although I can't remember it ever appearing on television in the end. At first I thought it was one of the funny things Victorians ate, but after thinking once again I became won over (like a dress on a rail that you think you wouldn't be seen dead in, but which looks nice when you try it on).

$1\frac{1}{2}$ pints (900 ml) milk

---

2 bay leaves

$1 \times \frac{1}{2}$ oz (15 g) sachet gelatine powder

---

4 egg yolks, beaten

---

caster sugar to taste

---

finely grated rind of 1 lemon

Put the milk and bay leaves into a saucepan and bring to the boil. Pour over the gelatine and stir to dissolve, then allow to cool. Strain the milk and stir in the egg yolks, a little caster sugar to taste and the lemon rind. Stir over a low heat until the custard thickens (or use a double saucepan) but do not let it boil. Remove from the heat and stir until nearly cold, then pour into a mould and leave to set.

Tia Maria Cream Junket

[SERVES 4]

I must admit, this nursery pudding used to meet with 'Ugh!' when it was made in the traditional way. I always felt the same until I worked with Mrs Cameron from the Isle of Mull. 'Eat it this way,' she said, and it makes quite a different pudding. It is a great improvement as the cream trickles down the side as you spoon away the junket, and I think I have made it even better by adding the Tia Maria or Bailey's to the cream!

---

1 pint (600 ml) milk

---

2 teaspoons caster sugar

---

a few drops of vanilla essence

---

liquid rennet according to the manufacturer's instructions

---

1 tablespoon Tia Maria or Bailey's Irish Cream

$\frac{1}{4}$ pint (150 ml) cream

---

a pinch of grated nutmeg

Warm the milk to blood heat, then stir in the sugar, vanilla essence and rennet. Pour into $\frac{1}{2}$ pint (300 ml) tumblers, leaving about 1 in (2.5 cm) space at the top, and leave them to set. Mix the Tia Maria or Bailey's into the cream and fill the tumblers to the top with cream. Sprinkle with grated nutmeg.

Ruth's Easy Trifle

[SERVES 4]

1 jam Swiss roll, cut into $\frac{1}{2}$ in (1 cm) rounds

1 × 11 oz (300 g) tin raspberries, drained and the juice reserved

2 tablespoons sherry or rum

2 tablespoons custard powder

1 tablespoon sugar

1 × 4 oz (400 g) tin evaporated milk made up to 1 pint (600 ml) with milk

$\frac{1}{2}$ pint (300 ml) double or whipping cream, lightly whipped

Lay the Swiss roll rounds in the bottom of a trifle dish and sprinkle with the raspberries. Mix the raspberry juice with the sherry or rum and spoon this over the Swiss roll. Leave to soak for 1 to 2 hours. Mix the custard powder and sugar with a little of the milk. Bring the remainder of the milk to almost boiling point, then stir it into the custard mixture. Return it to the heat and bring to the boil, stirring until it thickens. Allow the custard to cool a little, stirring to prevent a skin forming, then pour it over the dish, gently lifting the Swiss rolls up with a spoon as you do so to let the custard in and around them. When cold, cover with the lightly whipped cream, decorate with fruit or sugar strands and keep in the fridge until ready to serve.

Ginger Trifle

[SERVES 4]

This simple recipe is quick to make and even quicker to disappear! If you make it only an hour or so before serving, the biscuits stay nice and crunchy.

1 × 7 oz (1 × 200 g) packet ginger biscuits

$\frac{1}{2}$ pint (300 ml) double or whipping cream, whipped

1 × 11 oz (1 × 300 g) tin mandarin oranges, drained

2 tablespoons chopped mixed nuts

Place the biscuits in a bag and crush them with a rolling pin. In a glass bowl, place alternate layers of crumbled biscuits, whipped cream and mandarins, finishing with a layer of whipped cream. Sprinkle on the chopped nuts and serve.

One dessert the staff used to have regularly on Sunday nights was a whipped jelly. We made the jelly as usual, then when it was nearly set, whisked it with a rotary whisk and it came up like a mousse which was nice served with a bit of cream or a junket.

Caramel Custard

[SERVES 4]

This is a simple and delicious dessert which tastes lovely with fresh fruit salad or Orange Compote (see page 146). You can make it with milk instead of milk and cream if you prefer.

FOR THE CARAMEL:

6 oz (175 g) caster sugar

2 tablespoons water

FOR THE CUSTARD:

2 whole eggs

2 egg yolks

2 oz (50 g) caster sugar

½ pint (300 ml) milk

½ pint (300 ml) single cream

Put the sugar and water into a small saucepan and allow it to melt over a low heat without stirring. Watch it carefully, and when it begins to brown, give it a stir. When it is a nice brown, take it off the heat as it goes on cooking and pour it into a warmed soufflé dish. Wearing oven gloves or holding a cloth as the caramel is extremely hot, roll the caramel round the dish to coat the sides. Leave it to cool; you can listen to it crackle!

Pre-heat the oven to 325°F (160°C), gas mark 3. Mix the eggs, egg yolks and sugar in a mixing bowl. Heat the milk and cream but do not boil. Pour it on to the eggs, stir well, then pour it into the soufflé dish. Stand the dish in a roasting tin of cold water, cover with greaseproof paper and put it in the oven for about 1 hour until set. Allow it to go cold before turning it out of the dish.

I often used to sleep at Basildon House and it was a bit eerie at times because the house had all sorts of creaks and cracks. I was locking up one night when I heard what sounded like an army of feet on the gravel drive! I jumped into my car as quickly as I could, but it turned out to be an old horse who had got out of his field. He used to live over the other side of the grounds and was returning to his old haunts. After that, I heard him many times, but it gave me quite a turn!

Crème Brûlée

[SERVES 4]

This recipe is reputed to have come from Trinity College, Cambridge (though I doubt it was served to the students!). It is sometimes called Trinity College Pudding, and is lovely served with a fresh fruit salad or Orange Compote (see page 146).

4 egg yolks or 3 egg yolks and 1 egg

1 tablespoon caster sugar

1 pint (600 ml) single or double cream

a piece of vanilla pod, split open

2 oz (50 g) caster sugar for topping

Pre-heat the oven to 325°F (160°C), gas mark 3. Mix the egg yolks and sugar together well. Put the cream and vanilla pod in a double saucepan and bring almost to boiling point. Remove the vanilla pod and pour the cream on to the egg yolks, blending quickly and thoroughly. Return the mixture to the saucepan and thicken carefully over the heat, but do not allow to boil. Pour the mixture into a soufflé dish, leaving a space of about $\frac{1}{2}$ in (1 cm) at the top. Place the dish in a roasting tin and fill with water to come halfway up the dish. Cover with a piece of greaseproof paper and bake in the oven for about 1 hour until set, but do watch that it does not get too hot and overcook. I usually test by putting a thin-bladed knife into the centre to make sure that it is set. Take it out of the oven and leave it overnight.

Next day, cover the top with a thin even layer of caster sugar. Pre-heat the grill, and put the brûlée underneath for a few minutes to allow the sugar to become a light golden brown, then remove it from the heat and leave it in a cool place for 2 to 3 hours.

I generally use large eggs. Until recently, I used to buy a tray of cracks – 2$\frac{1}{2}$ dozen eggs of mixed sizes. They were much cheaper and always really fresh as you can't sell a stale cracked egg. But we are not allowed to buy them any more because of the fear of salmonella contamination.

Orange Compote

[SERVES 4]

This is a tasty dish, ideal for a party as it can be made the day before. It does take a bit of practice to segment the oranges, but it is well worth it.

4 large oranges

4 oz (100 g) caster sugar

3 tablespoons Grand Marnier or to taste

Remove the skin and pith from the oranges with a sharp knife. Slip the knife down one side of the membrane of the first segment, turn carefully and slide the segment out into a lidded bowl. Continue until you have removed all the segments. Squeeze any juice left in the skins over the oranges. Strain all the juice from the oranges, cover them with caster sugar and leave to stand for about 30 minutes. Drain off any more juice and add the Grand Marnier to taste – but don't be mean. Turn over the segments and put on the lid. Leave the oranges in the fridge and serve very cold with either Caramel Custard (see page 144) or, for preference, Crème Brûlée (see page 145).

Lemon Freezer Pudding

[SERVES 4]

This simple pudding is worth making and keeping in the freezer for unexpected guests or a quick dessert.

2 oz (50 g) digestive biscuits, crushed, or 2 oz (50 g) mixed nuts, finely ground

3 eggs, separated

4 oz (100 g) caster sugar

½ pint (300 ml) double cream

finely grated rind and juice of 2 lemons

nuts and glacé cherries to decorate

Grease a 2 pint (1.2 litre) loaf tin and cover the bottom and sides with biscuit crumbs or ground nuts. Whisk the egg whites until very stiff but not rocky, and gradually beat in the sugar. Reserve a little cream for decoration, then whisk the egg yolks and cream. Fold in the egg whites with the lemon rind and juice. Pour the mixture into the prepared tin and put in the fridge for about 1 hour until firm, then put it into the freezer. Remove from the freezer 15 minutes before serving and turn on to a serving dish. If it refuses to budge from the tin, hold the tin in warm water for a few seconds. Decorate with whipped cream, nuts and glacé cherries.

Raspberry or Strawberry Bavarois

[SERVES 4]

If raspberries or strawberries are in good condition, there is no better way to eat them than just as they are with caster sugar and a little cream. This is a good recipe if they are a little over-ripe.

12 oz (350 g) raspberries or strawberries
6 oz (175 g) icing sugar
juice of $\frac{1}{2}$ lemon
3 teaspoons gelatine powder
2 tablespoons hot water
$\frac{1}{2}$ pint (300 ml) double or whipping cream, whipped

Reserve a few raspberries or strawberries for decoration. Put the remainder into a food processor and process until smooth, then pass through a fine sieve to remove the pips. Turn the fruit purée into a bowl and add the icing sugar and lemon juice. Melt the gelatine in the hot water and add it to the mixture, stirring well. Allow to cool and when the mixture begins to thicken, fold in the whipped cream and turn into a serving dish. Decorate with the reserved fruit.

Creamy Chocolate Mousse

[SERVES 4]

Using more cream in this mousse makes it extra smooth, although you can use equal quantities of milk and cream. If you use a flake to decorate the top, it is much easier and less messy than grating chocolate.

$\frac{1}{4}$ pint (150 ml) milk
6 oz (175 g) plain chocolate or 2 tablespoons cocoa
3 eggs, separated
4 oz (100 g) caster sugar
$1 \times \frac{1}{2}$ oz (15 g) sachet gelatine powder
3 tablespoons hot water
$\frac{3}{4}$ pint (450 ml) double cream, whipped
1 chocolate flake

Put the milk and chocolate or cocoa in a small saucepan over a low heat to melt, then bring to boiling point. Beat the egg yolks and sugar until almost white, then pour on the flavoured milk and blend together. Return the mixture to the pan and allow to thicken over a low heat without boiling, then strain. Dissolve the gelatine in the hot water and add this to the mixture, stirring quickly. Leave to cool. Whisk the egg whites until stiff but not rocky. When the mousse is beginning to set round the edges, fold in the whipped cream and egg whites. Pour into a serving dish and leave in the fridge to set. Crumble the chocolate flake over the top.

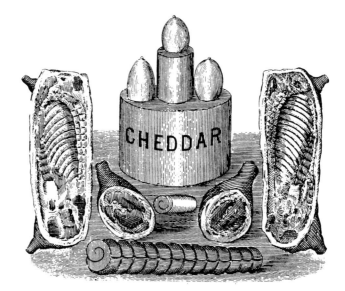

Part Eight

CHEESE AND OTHER SAVOURIES

Cheese Soufflé

[SERVES 4]

1 oz (25 g) unsalted butter
½ oz (15 g) plain flour
¼ pint (150 ml) milk
4 eggs, separated (only 3 yolks are needed)
salt and freshly ground black pepper
1½ oz (40 g) strong Cheddar cheese, grated
1½ oz (40 g) Parmesan cheese, grated

Don't use eggs that are too fresh for a soufflé, or they won't whip, and don't whip them rock hard. Make sure you mix a spoonful of whisked egg white with the cheese, then carefully fold in the remainder. This will make a nicer soufflé. Don't put it too high in the oven, either, or the top will 'crust' and will not allow the soufflé to rise.

Any soufflé must be served straight from the oven otherwise it will collapse, so your guests must wait for the soufflé, not the soufflé for the guests. Tell your guests that you are serving a soufflé, and they will be only too happy to be sitting at the table on time, ready to eat. I always tie a collar of greaseproof paper around the soufflé dish. When we had to walk through cool corridors from the kitchen to the dining room, we left the collar around the soufflé to protect it from draughts until the last possible moment, then whipped it off just before serving.

You can also cook the soufflé in ramekin dishes, but you may need a little practice.

Pre-heat the oven to 375 °F (190 °C), gas mark 5. Tie a collar of greaseproof paper around a greased 1 pint (600 ml) soufflé dish. Melt the butter in a saucepan, stir in the flour and cook the roux for about 1 minute. Gradually stir in the milk, bring to the boil and boil for 2 minutes. Allow to cool slightly, then beat in 3 egg yolks and season with salt and freshly ground black pepper. Whisk the 4 egg whites until firm. Stir in the cheese with a tablespoon of the whisked egg whites, then fold in the remaining egg whites. Turn the mixture into the prepared dish and bake in the centre of a moderate oven for about 20 minutes until well risen and golden brown. Serve immediately.

Cheesy Puff Rolls

Illustrated on page 156

[SERVES 4]

You can make your own pastry for these rolls or use frozen. Either way, they make a good buffet snack which I often used to serve at weddings.

---

8 oz (225 g) Puff Pastry (see page 201)

---

8 oz (225 g) Cheddar cheese

---

1 tablespoon chopped fresh parsley

---

freshly ground black pepper

---

1 egg, beaten

Pre-heat the oven to 425°F (220°C), gas mark 7. Roll out the pastry and cut into 3 in (7.5 cm) squares. Cut the cheese into small pieces and lay one on each pastry square. Sprinkle with chopped parsley and freshly ground black pepper. Moisten two opposite corners of the pastry and bring them up over the cheese, sealing them together to make a roll with the other two corners open. Place on a greased baking sheet and brush with beaten egg to glaze. Bake for about 10 minutes until the pastry is cooked and the cheese has melted out of the ends of the rolls.

Cheddary Prunes

[SERVES 4]

Tinned prunes are the easiest to use for this dish, but you can just as well use dried, cooked prunes. Try it with dates, too, for a change, or any cheese that you fancy. You can also serve chicken livers in the same way if you cut a slit in the centre for the cheese, but these take about 15 minutes to cook.

---

6 oz (175 g) mature Cheddar cheese

---

1 × 14 oz (400 g) tin stoned prunes, drained

---

8 oz (225 g) streaky bacon, rind removed

---

6 slices white bread

Pre-heat the oven to 400°F (200°C), gas mark 6. Cut the cheese into small chunks and push one into the centre of each prune. Cut the bacon into strips and wrap one round each prune. Place them on a baking tray and cook in the oven for about 10 minutes until the cheese has melted and the bacon is brown and crispy. Toast the bread, cut it into squares and lay the prunes on top to serve.

Ham and Cheese Dreams

[SERVES 4]

Use whatever cheese, ham or tongue you like for this simple snack.

8 thin slices white bread

6 oz (175 g) unsalted butter

1 tablespoon made mustard

4 slices ham

8 oz (225 g) Parmesan cheese, grated

Spread the bread with a little of the butter and then with mustard. Make into 4 sandwiches with the ham, then cut off the crusts and cut into fingers. Melt half the remaining butter and have it ready in a dish, and have the grated cheese ready in another. Dip the fingers into the butter, then the cheese. Heat some butter in a frying pan and fry the fingers until they are a nice golden brown on both sides.

Cheese Triangles

[MAKES ABOUT 20 BISCUITS]

This is a versatile recipe as you can use it to make the Cheese Triangles, or for plain cheese biscuits or cheese straws.

$3\frac{1}{2}$ oz (90 g) unsalted butter

6 oz (175 g) plain flour

$1\frac{1}{2}$ oz (40 g) Parmesan cheese, finely grated

salt and freshly ground black pepper

1 egg yolk, beaten or a little beaten egg

4 oz (100 g) cream cheese

stuffed olives, sliced hard-boiled egg, thinly sliced tomato and mustard and cress to garnish

Pre-heat the oven to 350°F (180°C), gas mark 4. Rub the fat into the flour until it resembles fine breadcrumbs. Mix in the grated cheese and season to taste with salt and freshly ground black pepper. Bind the mixture together with the egg yolk or beaten egg, and a spoonful of water if it does not bind well. Roll out into a rectangle and cut into triangles. Place them on a greased baking sheet and bake for about 15 minutes until a nice golden brown. Allow to cool, then pipe the cream cheese around the edges of the triangles and garnish with stuffed olives, hard-boiled egg, thinly sliced tomato and mustard and cress.

The Manor House in Yattendon in the 1930s. This is where I first started work.

OPPOSITE] *Coffee and Walnut Gâteau (page 141).*

*There's nothing to beat freshly baked bread
— and you don't have to bake it yourself . . . !*

OPPOSITE] *Cheesy Puff Rolls (page 151); Stilton Pâté (page 162).*
OVERLEAF] *German Iced Biscuits (page 188); Melting Moments (page 184);
Rum and Pineapple Cake (page 180).*

[*157*]

RUTH'S STORE CUPBOARD

I keep a selection of things in the store cupboard so I can always pep up a dish that needs a little something, or put together a new recipe.

In the sauces line, I keep Worcestershire sauce and pesto sauce, which is a strong basil sauce. I prefer it to dried basil; you never seem to lose that dead straw taste with dried herbs. Tubes of garlic paste, anchovy paste and tomato concentrate are useful too. Tins of tomato purée are wasteful, I find, because they go mouldy before you can use them up, but tins of beans and consommé often come in handy, plus a few packet soups.

A drop of sherry doesn't come amiss. And keeping a couple of cans of red and dry white wine, if your local shop sells them, saves opening a bottle when you only want a small amount. I don't bother to drink it, but how I love to throw it around the kitchen! I also keep some rum and brandy, Tia Maria, Crème de Menthe and Grand Marnier. I also make a sloe gin. When it's a good year for sloes, I pick a few extras and freeze them as you seldom get two good years straight off. Damsons can be used instead of sloes.

I like to use fresh herbs, but I generally have some dried oregano, which is nice in lasagne, and spices like cayenne pepper, cinnamon and nutmeg.

You can always knock up something if you have some nuts: walnuts, almonds and ground almonds, plus some dried fruit, coconut, black treacle and golden syrup, chocolate, a few Mars bars and a tin of condensed milk. Surprisingly, mashed potato powder can come in handy, too. Lemon Cheese (see page 175) keeps quite a while in the fridge, as does my Barbecue Sauce (see page 82). Egg whites go into meringues, so so I generally have some of those in a tin, and I keep some sticks of frozen cream in the freezer, perfect for taking out exactly how much you need. If I do have cream left over, I make a cheesecake and pop that in the freezer, as you can't freeze cream successfully at home. Part-baked baguettes or garlic rolls and frozen puff and filo pastry are also useful freezer standbys.

Cheese Scones

[MAKES 12 SCONES]

When you are making scones, pre-heat the baking tray and you will get lighter results.

8 oz (225 g) self-raising flour

½ teaspoon baking powder

a pinch of salt

2 oz (50 g) unsalted butter

4 oz (100 g) Cheddar cheese, grated

1 egg, beaten

2–3 tablespoons milk

Pre-heat the oven to 425°F (220°C), gas mark 7 and heat the baking sheet in the oven. Sift the flour, baking powder and salt into a mixing bowl and rub in the butter until the mixture resembles fine breadcrumbs. Stir in the cheese. Reserve a little of the egg, and beat the rest into the milk. Mix and knead it lightly into the dry ingredients to make a soft but not sticky dough. Roll out the dough to ½ in (1 cm) thick and cut out the scones with a 2 in (5 cm) cutter. Re-roll and cut the trimmings. Place the scones on the hot baking sheet, brush with the remaining beaten egg and bake for about 10 minutes until golden brown. Cool on a wire rack and serve buttered.

Stilton Pâté

Illustrated on page 156

[SERVES 4]

This makes an unusual addition to the cheese board, a tasty snack dish with crusty bread, or you can serve it with fingers of toast for an appetiser. It is a good way of using up the odd bits of Stilton you have over from your Christmas Stilton, or of using the bits inside the crust that you cut off from the cheese. You can make it as firm or as soft as you like by varying the quantities of the ingredients.

8 oz (225 g) Stilton, mashed

2 oz (50 g) unsalted butter

2 tablespoons brandy

2 tablespoons single or double cream

a few walnut halves to garnish

Mash the ingredients together thoroughly or process them, then press into pâté dishes and refrigerate. Turn out and top with a few walnut halves.

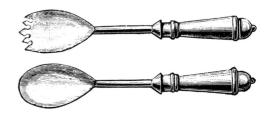

Cheese Mousse

[SERVES 4]

$\frac{1}{2}$ pint (300 ml) Béchamel Sauce (see page 194)

1 egg yolk

4 oz (100 g) mature Cheddar cheese, finely grated

salt and freshly ground black pepper

1 teaspoon mustard powder

1 tablespoon gelatine powder

3 tablespoons hot water

juice of $\frac{1}{2}$ lemon

$\frac{1}{4}$ pint (150 ml) double or whipping cream, whipped

3 egg whites, whipped

a sprig of watercress or sliced tomato to garnish

Make the béchamel sauce and allow it to cool. Beat in the egg yolk and grated cheese and season to taste with salt, freshly ground black pepper and mustard. Melt the gelatine in the water and add it to the sauce with the lemon juice. When it is just beginning to set, fold in the whipped cream and lastly the whipped egg whites. Turn into a glass soufflé dish and decorate with watercress leaves or slices of tomato. Serve well chilled with a green salad.

Camembert Ice-Cream

[SERVES 4]

1 whole ripe Camembert, rind removed

$\frac{1}{2}$ pint (300 ml) single cream

1 teaspoon salt

a few drops of tabasco sauce

1 teaspoon paprika

mustard and cress to garnish

Place the cheese and cream in a basin and beat to a liquid. Add salt and tabasco sauce to taste, pour into an ice-cream tray and freeze for at least 3 hours. When frozen, cut into fingers, sprinkle with paprika and place on a serving dish, garnished with mustard and cress. Serve with thin water biscuits.

Hard-boiled eggs make a useful savoury snack. You can cut them in half lengthways or across and cut a sliver off the base so that they stand up. Take out the yolks and mix them with chopped anchovies, sardines, curry powder, or grated cheese – in fact, whatever you fancy. Put the mixture back into the whites and serve on buttered brown bread cut into rounds and surrounded with shredded lettuce and watercress.

Egg Croquettes

[SERVES 4]

I often shape my croquettes like a cutlet. Then you can fry them in shallow oil, turning them over when the underside is cooked. If you are not keen on mushrooms or parsley, just leave them out.

---

1 oz (25 g) unsalted butter

1 oz (25 g) plain flour

8 fl oz (250 ml) milk

salt and freshly ground black pepper

4 hard-boiled eggs, roughly chopped

2 oz (50 g) mushrooms, chopped

1 tablespoon chopped fresh parsley

2 tablespoons plain flour

1 egg, beaten

4 oz (100 g) fresh white breadcrumbs

oil for deep frying

Melt the butter in a saucepan and stir in the flour. Cook for about 1 minute, then gradually stir in the milk to make a thick sauce. Season well with salt and freshly ground black pepper and continue to cook for about 2 minutes. Stir in the chopped eggs, mushrooms and parsley, and turn the mixture on to a plate to cool. Turn the mixture on to a floured board and make into a roll a bit thicker than a wine cork, then cut it into 2 in (5 cm) lengths. Roll them in a little more flour, coat them with beaten egg, then roll them in breadcrumbs. Heat the oil to 325°F (160°C) and fry the croquettes for about 4 minutes until golden brown.

I love poached eggs as a snack or a light meal. I don't use a poacher but boil some water with a dash of lemon or vinegar. If you stir the water round and round with a spoon before you add the egg, it will wind up and roll over in a ball. You do need really fresh eggs, though, and you can test them by putting them into a bowl of cold water. If they lie horizontally on the bottom, they are fresh; if they float upright, they are not. I'm not sure what happens if they go halfway!

Creamed Haddock on Toast

[SERVES 4]

Smoked haddock is a particular favourite of mine, and the better the haddock, the better the taste of this dish.

---

8 oz (225 g) smoked haddock

¼ pint (150 ml) double cream

---

freshly ground black pepper

Pre-heat the oven to 350°F (180°C), gas mark 4. Flake the haddock into the cream and season with lots of freshly ground black pepper. Put into the oven for about 15 minutes to heat through and serve on hot crisp toast.

If you are lucky enough to find some fresh herring roes, wash them well and take out the red string membrane; this helps to stop the roes curling up. Put them on a well-buttered baking sheet in a hot oven at 425°F (220°C), gas mark 7, for about 10 minutes, or under the grill. Serve on hot buttered toast. You will need 2 roes per person.

Scotch Woodcock

[SERVES 4]

This is a quick dish which can be served as a snack or as an entrée. Go easy with the salt in the eggs as Gentleman's Relish is quite salty.

---

4 slices bread

---

4 oz (100 g) unsalted butter

Gentleman's Relish

---

6 eggs, beaten

---

1 tablespoon single cream

---

salt and freshly ground black pepper

Toast the bread, then spread it with butter and Gentleman's Relish. Melt a little butter in a saucepan and lightly scramble the eggs and cream, seasoning lightly to taste with salt and freshly ground black pepper. Work in another knob of butter to keep the eggs shiny and moist. Spread the eggs over the toast and cut into fingers. Serve immediately.

Part Nine

PICKLES AND CHUTNEYS

Pickled Onions or Shallots

[MAKES 6 LB (2.75 KG) ONIONS]

This old pub recipe was given to me about forty years ago. It often brings tears to the eyes, but is well worth it. I never soak my onions in brine as it makes them too sharp. Just prepare them and hurtle them straight into the jar. I use a large glass sweet jar with a plastic lid with several pieces of greaseproof paper inside. I know it is a popular recipe because I have to keep mine in the woodshed so they don't all disappear at once. You can, of course, prepare your own spiced vinegar, but it is so easy to buy it already made. Be sure to make it as given, as the acid in the vinegar makes the sugar and vinegar emulsify.

7 lb (3 kg) pickling onions or shallots

2 tablespoons demerara sugar

2 tablespoons black treacle

4 pints (2.25 litres) pickling vinegar

Forget about peeling the onions dry. Put them in a bowl of water, peel them and drop them straight into the jars. Add the demerara sugar and treacle and pour over the cold spiced vinegar, making sure the onions are covered. Cover with air-tight vinegar-proof tops. Store for about 2 months before eating.

I like to make my own pickles and chutneys, and tend to put in whatever is around at the time. It can be a good way to use up over-ripe fruits. Chutneys need either long, slow boiling, or I sometimes pop them in the oven and then just finish them off on the hotplate – it saves a lot of stirring! Of course, you need to make sure you cook them in a suitable flameproof casserole. Never boil chutneys in a copper pan, and it is best to avoid aluminium, too, as some fruits can react with the metal. Stainless steel is the best. You need to pour the chutney into warmed glass jars when it is ready. I find coffee jars are ideal for bottling chutneys as they screw tight and the lids are plastic; never use metal lids for any pickles as the vinegar will react with the metal.

Pickled Oranges

[MAKES ABOUT I LB (450 G)]

These make a nice change served with pork, duck, chicken or turkey. The quantity depends on the size of your oranges; it doesn't really matter.

6 thin-skinned oranges, cut across into $\frac{1}{4}$ in (5 mm) slices
water
$1\frac{1}{2}$ pints (900 ml) white vinegar
$1\frac{1}{2}$ lb (750 g) granulated sugar
2 teaspoons ground cloves
$1\frac{1}{2}$ in (4 cm) cinnamon stick
a few whole cloves

Place the oranges in a large saucepan with just enough water to cover, bring to the boil, then simmer them for about 45 minutes until the rind is soft. Remove the rings carefully, then add the vinegar, sugar, ground cloves and cinnamon to the pan. Bring back to the boil and simmer for 15 minutes. Return a few orange rings at a time to the pan and cook for about 10 minutes until the rind becomes transparent. Lift the orange rings from the syrup into pre-heated jars. When they have all been cooked, boil the remaining syrup for about 15 minutes until it begins to thicken. Leave it to cool, then pour it over the orange rings, adding a few of the whole cloves to each jar. Cover with air-tight, vinegar-proof tops.

Pickled Eggs

[MAKES 6 EGGS]

After eating my pickled onions, I always keep the vinegar and use that for pickling eggs. The eggs take on a darkish brown look but have a pleasant flavour.

---

6 hard-boiled eggs, shelled

---

1 pint (600 ml) pickling vinegar or cider vinegar with 1 oz (25 g) pickling spice

---

If you use ready spiced pickling vinegar, you only need to pour it over the cooked eggs. With cider vinegar, bring it to the boil with the spices, then allow it to get cold before you pour it over the eggs. Whichever method you use, seal the jars with air-tight and vinegar-proof tops. Leave for about 2 weeks before eating.

I like to keep some herb wine vinegars for cooking. I just push a sprig of what I like into a bottle of white wine vinegar, but I think tarragon vinegar is my favourite.

Pickled Red Cabbage

[MAKES 3 ½ LB (1.5 KG)]

This makes a delicious crisp pickle, but do use it within about 3 weeks otherwise the cabbage begins to go limp.

---

3 lb (1.5 kg) red cabbage, finely shredded and stump removed

---

2 large onions, peeled and sliced

---

3 tablespoons salt

---

4 pints (2.25 litres) pickling vinegar

---

1 tablespoon soft brown sugar

Place the cabbage and onions in layers in a large basin, sprinkling each layer with some of the salt. Leave overnight. Next day, rinse off the salt and drain again. Pack into jars. Heat the vinegar and stir in the sugar until it dissolves. Then bring the vinegar to the boil, remove it from the heat and leave it to get cold. Pour it over the cabbage and onion and cover with air-tight and vinegar-proof tops.

Green Tomato Chutney

[MAKES ABOUT 4 LB (1.75 KG)]

I always cook chutneys in a flameproof casserole in the oven, then finish them off on the top of the stove when they are almost cooked. Otherwise you have to keep on stirring them for hours!

3 lb (1.5 kg) green tomatoes, sliced
1 lb (450 g) onions, sliced
salt
1 lb (450 g) soft brown sugar
1 teaspoon cayenne pepper
½ teaspoon ground ginger
2 lb (1 kg) apples, peeled, cored and chopped
8 oz (225 g) sultanas, chopped
2 oz (50 g) mustard seeds
1 pint (600 ml) vinegar

Spread the tomatoes and onions separately in two large dishes, cover with a good sprinkling of salt and leave to stand for 12 hours to draw out the juices. Drain well.

Pre-heat the oven to 350°F (180°C), gas mark 4. Put all the ingredients in a large flameproof casserole and bring to the boil. Put the casserole in the oven for about 2 hours. When the chutney is beginning to thicken, return it to the top of the stove, and boil, stirring continuously, for about 20 minutes until it has thickened and looks like jam. Allow to cool, then bottle and seal with air-tight and vinegar-proof tops. The chutney can be eaten after about 2 weeks.

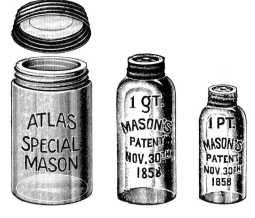

Pepper and Tomato Chutney

[MAKES ABOUT 3 LB (1.5 KG)]

This pepper and tomato chutney is especially good served with cold meat and salad.

---

2 red peppers, deseeded and chopped

2 green peppers, deseeded and chopped

2 yellow peppers, deseeded and chopped

1 lb (450 g) ripe tomatoes, skinned and chopped

12 oz (350 g) onions, chopped

8 oz (225 g) demerara sugar

1 pint (600 ml) malt vinegar

1 teaspoon allspice
1 teaspoon mustard seeds
2 teaspoons black peppercorns } tied in a muslin bag

Place all the ingredients except the spices in a large saucepan and heat gently until the sugar dissolves. Add the spices in the muslin bag, bring to the boil and simmer gently for about 1½ hours until thick and pulpy. Remove and discard the muslin bag. Pour into warmed jars and seal with air-tight and vinegar-proof tops.

Beetroot Chutney

[MAKES ABOUT 4 LB (1.75 KG)]

This is a favourite WI recipe which makes a nice change from beetroot in vinegar.

1½ lb (750 g) raw beetroot, peeled and coarsely grated

1 lb (450 g) cooking apples, peeled, cored and chopped

8 oz (225 g) onions, chopped

8 oz (225 g) raisins

1¼ lb (500 g) granulated sugar

1¼ pints (750 ml) malt vinegar

1 teaspoon ground ginger

juice of ½ lemon

Place all the ingredients in a preserving pan and bring to the boil. Simmer gently, uncovered, for 2½ hours, stirring occasionally, until there is no excess liquid and the mixture is thick. Pour into warmed jars and cover immediately with air-tight and vinegar-proof tops.

Quick Uncooked Chutney

[MAKES ABOUT 6 LB (2.75 KG)]

This is an easy recipe which avoids that smell of vinegar you get in the kitchen when you are making chutney. I chop my ingredients by hand so that they are not too fine, but you can use a processor if you are careful.

---

4 lb (1.75 kg) cooking apples, peeled, cored and chopped (weigh after preparing)

---

1 lb (450 g) shallots, chopped

---

1 lb (450 g) sultanas, chopped

---

1 lb (450 g) stoned dates, chopped

---

1 oz (25 g) ground ginger

---

2 oz (50 g) salt

---

1 teaspoon chilli powder

1½ pints (900 ml) malt vinegar

Mix all the ingredients together well, then bottle and seal with air-tight and vinegar-proof tops.

Plum Chutney

[MAKES ABOUT 6 LB (2.75 KG)]

---

1 oz (25 g) pickling spice tied in a muslin bag or 1 sachet pickling spice

---

2 lb (1 kg) plums, halved, stoned and chopped

---

8 oz (225 g) red tomatoes, skinned and chopped

1½ pints (900 ml) malt vinegar

---

1 lb (450 g) onions, chopped

---

1 lb (450 g) cooking apples, peeled, cored and chopped (weigh after preparing)

---

8 oz (225 g) sultanas

---

1 lb (450) demerara sugar

---

1 tablespoon salt

Place all the ingredients in a preserving pan, bring to the boil and simmer for about 2½ hours, stirring occasionally, until thick. Remove and discard the pickling spice. Pour the chutney into warmed jars, cover and seal immediately with air-tight and vinegar-proof tops.

Crab Apple and Rosemary Jelly

[MAKES ABOUT 4 LB (1.75 KG)]

We used to make chutneys and jellies in vast quantities in the big houses where I worked. If the gardener had a surplus of something, it could never be wasted. We always used windfalls for apple jelly, which goes well with lamb and pork, but is good with whatever you fancy. You can use ordinary cooking apples, but crab apples are particularly nice as they cook to such a lovely rosy colour.

You can use any herbs for the jelly – mint, parsley, sage, thyme, rosemary – although rosemary and mint are probably the most popular. Blanching them makes the leaves go nice and green. Do be careful with the rosemary, or if you use sage or thyme, as these are all very strong herbs.

4 lb (1.75 g) crab apples

3 pints (1.75 litres) water

sugar (see method)

2 sprigs rosemary, or to taste

Remove any bruised parts from the apples, but do not peel or core them. Wash them well, then chop them into chunks and put into a large saucepan with just enough water to cover. Bring to the boil and simmer for about 30 minutes until reduced to a pulp. Turn into a jelly bag, or make a 'Dick Whittington' bag with a clean tea cloth or piece of sheeting. Hang it up over a bowl to drip overnight. Do not squeeze the bag or the jelly will be cloudy.

Measure the juice and add 1 lb (450 g) sugar to each 1 pint (600 ml) of liquid. Place the juice and sugar in a saucepan and stir over a moderate heat until the sugar has dissolved. Bring to the boil and boil rapidly for about 10 minutes until setting point is reached at 220°F (104°C). If you do not have a jam thermometer, put a spoonful on to a saucer and leave to cool. If a finger drawn across the jam makes it wrinkle, then it is ready. Pick off the rosemary leaves and blanch them in boiling water for a few seconds, then dry on kitchen paper and chop. Stir into the jelly to taste, then bottle and seal with air-tight lids.

Lemon Cheese

[MAKES ABOUT 2 LB (1 KG)]

Once again, this is Mott's way of saving lots of time stirring! I always keep a pot in the fridge as it makes a nice filling for sponge cakes and is good in tartlets with some strawberry jam on the bottom, then a layer of lemon cheese, topped with some whipped cream.

8 oz (225 g) unsalted butter

8 oz (225 g) caster sugar

coarsely grated rind and juice of 3 lemons

3 large eggs

Place the butter, sugar, grated lemon rind and juice in a double saucepan with boiling water in the base. Make the mixture fairly hot, stirring now and again to dissolve the sugar. Beat the eggs in a bowl, and gradually work in the hot mixture. Return the mixture to the saucepan and stir until the mixture thickens and coats the back of the wooden spoon. Remove from the heat and put through a strainer to remove the bits of rind. Pour into jars and allow to cool, then store in the fridge.

JELLIES AND JAMS

I like to make jams with whatever fruits are available, and the general rule is equal quantities of fruit to sugar, plus water according to the fruit. Quince jam is a particular favourite as it has a sharp flavour and goes well with meats like pork. It doesn't set very well, though, so instead of adding a bottle of pectin, which has no flavour, I make it with my Apply Jelly instead of water. It is a good idea for any fruits that don't set well – rhubarb or cherries, for example.

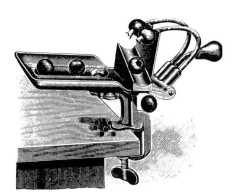

Part Ten

TEATIME RECIPES

Date and Orange Loaf

[MAKES 1 × 2 LB (1 KG) CAKE]

A nice teatime recipe which is good on its own or with butter.

8 oz (225 g) sugar-rolled chopped dates
4 fl oz (120 ml) water
6 oz (175 g) dark soft brown sugar
3 oz (75 g) hard margarine
grated rind of 1 orange
3 tablespoons orange juice
1 egg, beaten
1 teaspoon ground cinnamon
8 oz (225 g) self-raising flour

Pre-heat the oven to 350°F (180°C), gas mark 4. Put the dates and water in a saucepan, bring to the boil and simmer for about 10 minutes until pulpy. Add the sugar and stir until dissolved. Remove from the heat and beat in the margarine. Add the grated orange rind and juice, then allow to cool and beat in the egg. Sieve the cinnamon and flour together and add, a little at a time, to the date mixture. Beat well, then turn into a greased 2 lb (1 kg) loaf tin and bake for about 1 hour. If the loaf is not quite ready, return it to the oven for an extra 10 minutes.

Moist Fruit Cake

[MAKES 1 × 8 IN (20 CM) CAKE]

I find this cake always seems to rise evenly, and keeps very moist. If I want to make it for a special occasion, I substitute sherry or rum for the water. Made early in December, it can be iced for Christmas.

4 oz (100 g) hard margarine
8 oz (225 g) soft brown sugar
1 lb (450 g) dried mixed fruit
$\frac{1}{4}$ pint (150 ml) water
2 eggs, beaten
8 oz (225 g) self-raising flour

Pre-heat the oven to 300°F (150°C), gas mark 2. Put the margarine, sugar, fruit and water into a saucepan, bring to the boil and simmer, covered, for 15 minutes. Allow to cool, then add the eggs and flour and turn the mixture into a greased and lined 8 in (20 cm) cake tin. Bake for 1½ to 2 hours until the cake is brown on top and beginning to come away from the sides of the tin.

Victorian Seed Cake

[MAKES 1 × 10 IN (25 CM) CAKE]

We made this cake for *The Victorian Kitchen* television series. The sprinkling of caster sugar on the top gives it a nice gooey crust.

1 lb (450 g) unsalted butter
1 lb (450 g) caster sugar
1 lb (450 g) self-raising flour
2 oz (50 g) cornflour
1 oz (25 g) caraway seeds
10 eggs, separated
1 tablespoon caster sugar

Pre-heat the oven to 350°F (180°C), gas mark 4. Cream the butter and sugar together until pale and fluffy, then fold in the flour and cornflour. Add the caraway seeds. Beat the egg yolks and mix them into the flour mixture. Whisk the whites until fairly stiff and gently fold them into the mixture. Pour into a greased and lined 10 in (25 cm) cake tin and sprinkle the top with a tablespoon of caster sugar. Bake for $1\frac{1}{2}$ to 2 hours until the top is golden brown and the cake starts to come away from the sides of the tin.

Sticky Gingerbread

[MAKES 1 × 8 IN (20 CM) CAKE]

This cake improves if kept for about a week.

2 oz (50 g) black treacle
2 oz (50 g) golden syrup
4 oz (100 g) hard margarine
4 oz (100 g) soft brown sugar
1 tablespoon ground ginger
1 teaspoon ground cinnamon
6 oz (175 g) plain flour
1 egg, beaten
$\frac{1}{4}$ pint (150 ml) milk
1 teaspoon bicarbonate of soda
2 oz (50 g) sultanas (optional)

Pre-heat the oven to 350°F (180°C), gas mark 4. Put the treacle, syrup, margarine and sugar into a saucepan and stir over a low heat until just melted. Mix together the ground ginger, cinnamon and flour, add the egg and stir this into the syrup mixture. Heat the milk to lukewarm, then pour it over the bicarbonate of soda and stir this into the mixture. Add the sultanas, if using. Turn into a greased and lined 8 in (20 cm) square cake tin and bake for about 1 hour. Allow to cool in the tin, then wrap in foil.

Morning Star Mud Cake

[MAKES 1 × 8 IN (20 CM) CAKE]

This is another recipe borrowed from a local pub. It makes ever such a sticky gooey mess!

---

8 oz (225 g) unsalted butter

---

8 oz (225 g) plain chocolate

---

8 oz (225 g) caster sugar

---

4 eggs, lightly beaten

---

1 heaped teaspoon cornflour

Pre-heat the oven to 350°F (180°C), gas mark 4. Melt the butter and chocolate, then mix them into the sugar. Gradually mix in the eggs and fold in the cornflour. Turn the mixture into a greased and lined 8 in (20 cm) cake tin and stand it in a roasting tin filled with water to come halfway up the sides of the cake tin. Bake for about 1 hour, then leave to cool in the tin and refrigerate before turning out.

Rum and Pineapple Cake

Illustrated on page 159

[MAKES 1 × 8 IN (20 CM) CAKE]

When using glacé cherries, I split them in half, wash them well in warm water and dry them carefully. Then I dust them with a little flour. If you do this they usually stay 'up' in the cake.

---

5 oz (150 g) unsalted butter

---

4 oz (100 g) caster sugar

---

2 large eggs, beaten

---

8 oz (225 g) self-raising flour

¼ teaspoon baking powder

¼ teaspoon ground cinnamon

---

7 oz (200 g) sultanas

---

1 oz (25 g) glacé cherries, finely chopped

---

1 × 14 oz (400 g) tin pineapple, drained and finely chopped

---

2 tablespoons dark rum

---

icing sugar for dusting

Pre-heat the oven to 325°F (160°C), gas mark 3. Cream the butter and sugar until light and fluffy. Add the eggs, one at a time, beating in a tablespoonful of flour with each addition. Fold in the remaining flour, baking powder and cinnamon. Stir in the sultanas, chopped glacé cherries and pineapple and add the rum. Turn into a greased 8 in (20 cm) cake tin and bake for 1 to 1½ hours. Cool on a wire tray and dust with icing sugar before serving.

Greta's Almond Cake

[MAKES 1 × 8 IN (20 CM) CAKE]

A Swedish visitor first made this cake for us, and we have kept the recipe ever since. It is a light cake with a good texture which slices nicely. Make sure you do not overwhip the egg whites, otherwise it can make the cake heavy.

7 oz (200 g) unsalted butter

7 oz (200 g) caster sugar

4 eggs, separated

7 oz (200 g) self-raising flour

2 oz (50 g) almonds, chopped

½ oz (15 g) grated orange rind

2 oz (50 g) currants

Pre-heat the oven to 350°F (180°C), gas mark 4. Cream the butter and sugar until light and fluffy. Add the beaten egg yolks. Fold in the flour, chopped almonds, orange rind and currants. Whip the whites until stiff but not rocky and gently fold them into the mixture, then turn it into a greased 8 in (20 cm) cake tin and bake for about 1 hour.

Mrs Corrie's Chocolate Cake

[MAKES 1 × 7 IN (18 CM) CAKE]

This is a simple refrigerated cake which is very moreish!

8 oz (225 g) milk chocolate

8 oz (225 g) unsalted butter

2 eggs, beaten

2 teaspoons caster sugar

8 oz (225 g) Nice or Rich Tea biscuits, crushed

1 tablespoon chopped mixed nuts

Melt the chocolate and butter separately. Beat the eggs with the caster sugar, then mix in the chocolate and butter. Add the crushed biscuits and chopped nuts. Press into a greased 7 in (18 cm) spring-form cake tin and refrigerate overnight.

I always cook one cake at a time for best results because there is such a temperature variation when you have more than one thing in the oven. All ovens are different, too, so it pays to get to know your own. When I was cooking at some houses, I used to go an hour earlier to allow for the oven!

Moist Chocolate Cake with Coffee Filling

[MAKES 1 × 7 IN (18 CM) CAKE]

You can split and fill this cake with whipped cream, but I like it best with coffee butter icing.

6 oz (175 g) self-raising flour
2 oz (50 g) cocoa
8 oz (225 g) margarine
4 oz (100 g) caster sugar
4 oz (100 g) black treacle
4 eggs, beaten
1 oz (25 g) granulated sugar

FOR THE FILLING:

4 oz (100 g) unsalted butter
8 oz (225 g) icing sugar, sifted
2 to 3 teaspoons coffee essence

Pre-heat the oven to 325°F (160°C), gas mark 3. Sift the flour and cocoa together. Cream the margarine and sugar until light and fluffy, then mix in the treacle and gradually add the eggs, beating well after each addition. Add a teaspoon of the flour mixture if it looks like curdling. Fold in the flour and cocoa and spread evenly in a greased and lined 7 in (18 cm) cake tin. Bake just below the centre of the oven for about 1 hour. Remove the cake from the oven and sprinkle with the granulated sugar, then return it to the oven for a further 30 minutes. The cake is done when it begins to shrink from the sides of the tin and the centre springs back when pressed with a finger. Leave to cool for 15 minutes before removing from the tin and taking off the paper. Allow to cool completely on a wire rack before filling with butter icing.

To make the filling, cream the butter until soft, then beat in the icing sugar and coffee essence. Split the cake in half and fill with the coffee icing.

The staff often used to enjoy most of the cakes and biscuits we made for teas, as the ladies who were invited to afternoon teas rarely ate a great deal; sometimes they went to more than one house in the afternoon. They always kept their hats on and I can remember the hostess dashing upstairs before her guests arrived to put on her afternoon hat. The cakes had to be served uncut to show that they were made specially for the occasion, so you could not save a cake for entertaining the next day if someone had tried it. You could always recognise the upper classes by the way they had their tea poured. Types like me always put the milk in first, but putting the tea in first was a sign of class!

Walnut Brownies

[MAKES ABOUT 16 BROWNIES]

I always keep plenty of cakes in the house as I mostly have six or eight of the family on Sundays and they go through my tins to find out what I have baked during the week! Do use granulated sugar for this recipe to get the best texture.

---

8 oz (225 g) granulated sugar

---

4 oz (100 g) unsalted butter, melted

---

4 oz (100 g) self-raising flour

---

4 oz (100 g) walnuts, chopped

---

4 oz (100 g) plain chocolate, melted

---

2 eggs, beaten

Pre-heat the oven to 350°F (180°C), gas mark 4. Mix the sugar and melted butter, fold in the flour and chopped walnuts, then stir in the melted chocolate and beaten eggs. Pour the mixture into a greased and lined 8 in (20 cm) square cake tin and bake for about 30 minutes until firm. Mark into squares and allow to cool slightly before removing from the tin.

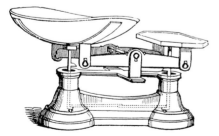

Almond Slices

[MAKES ABOUT 10 FINGERS]

These almond slices were often served with afternoon tea at the big houses.

---

4 oz (100 g) unsalted butter

---

8 oz (225 g) plain flour

---

1 teaspoon baking powder

---

2 oz (50 g) caster sugar

---

1 egg yolk

---

4 tablespoons apricot jam

---

1 egg white

---

3 oz (75 g) icing sugar

---

3 oz (75 g) slivered almonds

Pre-heat the oven to 325°F (160°C), gas mark 3. Rub the butter into the flour and baking powder until the mixture resembles fine breadcrumbs, then add the sugar and bind the mixture to a stiff consistency with the egg yolk. Knead well, then roll into a long strip about $\frac{1}{4}$ in (5 mm) thick. Cut into 3 and place on a greased baking tray, prick with a fork and make a small lip along both edges. Spread with the apricot jam. Whisk the egg white until frothy, then gradually stir in the icing sugar. Spread over the jam and sprinkle with the chopped almonds. Bake for 50 to 60 minutes until golden brown. Allow to cool for a few minutes before cutting into fingers.

Flapjacks

[MAKES ABOUT 16 CAKES]

These flapjacks are so easy to make and always go down well with adults and children.

3 oz (75 g) unsalted butter
1½ tablespoons golden syrup
6 oz (175 g) porridge oats
a pinch of salt
1½ oz (40 g) light brown sugar

Pre-heat the oven to 350°F (180°C), gas mark 4. Melt the butter with the syrup, but do not allow the mixture to boil. Mix in the oats, salt and sugar and press into a greased 8 in (20 cm) square cake tin. Bake for about 20 minutes until golden brown. Cut into squares while still hot, then allow to cool before removing from the tin.

Melting Moments

Illustrated on page 158

[MAKES ABOUT 20 CAKES]

These are delicious light little cakes – easy to make and, as the name suggests, they melt in your mouth.

2½ oz (65 g) lard
1½ oz (40 g) margarine
3 oz (75 g) caster sugar
½ egg, beaten
a few drops of vanilla essence
5 oz (150 g) self-raising flour
4 tablespoons porridge oats
10 glacé cherries, halved

Pre-heat the oven to 350°F (180°C), gas mark 4. Cream the lard and margarine with the sugar until light and fluffy. Beat in the egg and vanilla essence and fold in the flour. Roll the mixture into small balls with wet hands, then coat them in the oats. Place the cakes on a greased baking tray, allowing room for them to spread, and put a cherry half on the top of each one. Press them lightly with your finger to flatten them. Bake for about 15 to 20 minutes and allow to cool on the tray.

Walnut Sablets

[MAKES ABOUT 12 SABLETS]

An unusual and tasty biscuit, Walnut Sablets make a nice teatime treat.

4 oz (100 g) unsalted butter

4 oz (100 g) cornflour

2 oz (50 g) caster sugar

1 tablespoon sherry

1 egg yolk

FOR THE TOPPING:

1 egg white

1 oz (25 g) caster sugar

2 oz (50 g) walnuts, chopped

Pre-heat the oven to 325°F (160°C), gas mark 3. Rub the butter into the cornflour until the mixture resembles fine breadcrumbs. Add the sugar and sherry and enough egg yolk to make a stiff consistency. Roll out to about $\frac{1}{8}$ in (3 mm) thick, cut into crescents or strips and place on a greased baking tray. Beat the egg white until frothy, then beat in the sugar. Spread the topping over the biscuits and sprinkle with chopped walnuts. Bake for about 20 to 30 minutes until the biscuits are crisp and the topping is firm.

Coconut Finger Biscuits

[MAKES ABOUT 20 BISCUITS]

I like to make these with a coconut which is not too fine so that the biscuits have a good texture.

3 oz (75 g) unsalted butter

6 oz (175 g) plain flour

3 oz (75 g) desiccated coconut

$1\frac{1}{2}$ oz (40 g) caster sugar

1 egg yolk

a little water if necessary

3 tablespoons strawberry or raspberry jam

egg white to glaze

Pre-heat the oven to 350°F (180°C), gas mark 4. Rub the butter into the flour until the mixture resembles fine breadcrumbs. Add 2 oz (50 g) of the coconut and the sugar and mix together with the egg yolk and a little water if necessary to make the pastry the consistency of shortcrust. Divide into 2 and roll out to rectangles about $\frac{1}{4}$ in (5 mm) thick. Place one half on a greased baking tray, prick with a fork and spread thinly with jam. Cover with the other half. Brush with egg white, cut into fingers and scatter the remaining coconut over the top. Bake for about 15 to 20 minutes until cooked.

Viennese Shortcakes

[MAKES ABOUT 10 CAKES]

I find these are a special favourite with the young ones.

---

6 oz (175 g) unsalted butter

1½ oz (40 g) caster sugar

a few drops of vanilla essence

6 oz (175 g) plain flour

icing sugar for dusting

2 tablespoons strawberry or raspberry jam

Pre-heat the oven to 325°F (160°C), gas mark 3. Cream the butter and sugar until very light and fluffy, then add one or two drops of vanilla essence. Gradually add the sieved flour and mix until smooth. Put the mixture into a piping bag with a large star nozzle. Pipe the mixture into paper bun cases, keeping well to the outside so you have an indentation in the centre when the cakes are baked. Bake for about 30 minutes, then allow to cool. Dust with icing sugar and put a little red jam in the centre.

Ruth's Shortbread

[MAKES 1 × 8 IN (20 CM) SHORTBREAD]

I break all the rules with this recipe, but it is easy and delicious!

---

4 oz (100 g) unsalted butter

2 oz (50 g) caster sugar

8 oz (225 g) plain flour

Pre-heat the oven to 300°F (150°C), gas mark 2. Soften the butter, beat it until it is very soft, then work in the sugar with your hand. Finally work in the flour, still with your hand. If you cannot work in all the flour, don't worry, as long as you don't have more than 1 oz (25 g) over. Roll out the mixture to about ½ in (1 cm) thick and cut it into fingers, or make it into a round and mark it into 8 wedges. Prick all over with a fork, then bake for 30 to 40 minutes until just coloured. Leave to cool in the tin for about 2 minutes, then put a knife right through the markings and leave for a further 5 minutes before lifting on to a wire rack to finish cooling.

When I went out to work my mum thought I'd be better off if I didn't drink because of all the men in the houses, and I never have, except the occasional glass of white wine. But I do like others to have a drink, and I could acquire quite a good taste for Champagne, I think! Lord Iliffe always laughs because he says, 'You don't drink do you, Mrs Mott?' and I say, 'No, but I do like Champagne!'

I like to cook with wine and spirits, too. Rum is a favourite because it has a stronger flavour in cooking than brandy. Brandy can curdle so quickly, whereas rum is much easier to handle and has a lovely toffee smell.

To make your mince pies extra special, serve them with some rum butter. Cream 3 oz (75 g) unsalted butter, beat in 5 oz (150 g) caster or icing sugar and the grated rind of half an orange, then beat in 2 to 3 tablespoons of rum. The best way to eat them is to get the pies hot, then carefully lift the lid when serving and pop in a spoonful of the rum butter. This begins to melt and tastes great, but keep your chin over the plate!

Sara's Ginger Snaps

[MAKES ABOUT 36 BISCUITS]

This is another of my niece Sara's recipes; a simple and tasty family favourite.

2 oz (50 g) margarine
4 oz (100 g) caster sugar
1 tablespoon golden syrup
$1\frac{1}{2}$ tablespoons lightly beaten egg
6 oz (175 g) self-raising flour
1 teaspoon ground ginger
1 teaspoon bicarbonate of soda

Pre-heat the oven to 350°F (180°C), gas mark 4. Cream the margarine, sugar and syrup. Gradually beat in the egg. Then stir in the dry ingredients until the mixture forms a soft dough. Roll out into a sausage shape and cut into 36 pieces about 1 in (2.5 cm) long. Roll into balls, place on a greased baking tray, flatten gently and bake for 10 to 15 minutes until crispy and brown. Cool on a wire rack.

German Iced Biscuits

Illustrated on page 158

[MAKES ABOUT 8 BISCUITS]

An unusual and tasty recipe, this one is well worth the effort.

2 oz (50 g) unsalted butter

4 oz (100 g) plain flour

1 oz (25 g) caster sugar

4 tablespoons redcurrant jelly

FOR THE GLACÉ ICING:

1–2 tablespoons lemon juice

4 oz (100 g) icing sugar

4 glacé cherries, halved

Pre-heat the oven to 350°F (180°C) gas mark 4. Rub the butter into the flour until the mixture resembles fine breadcrumbs, then add the sugar and knead into a smooth paste. Roll out to $\frac{1}{4}$ in (5 mm) thick and cut into rounds. Place on a greased baking tray and bake for about 10 minutes until golden brown. When cold, sandwich together with redcurrant jelly. Mix the lemon juice gradually into the icing sugar until the mixture is thick enough to coat the back of a spoon. Spread the icing over the biscuits and top with half a glacé cherry.

Drop Scones

[MAKES ABOUT 10 SCONES]

Drop scones are best eaten with butter and jam on the day they are made.

8 oz (225 g) plain flour

1 tablespoon caster sugar

1 egg

$\frac{1}{2}$ pint (300 ml) milk

1 teaspoon bicarbonate of soda

2 teaspoons cream of tartar

lard for greasing

Mix the flour and sugar and make a well in the centre. Break in the egg and beat in the milk until you have a thick batter. Beat in the bicarbonate of soda and cream of tartar just before using. Heat up a griddle or large heavy frying pan and grease it with a little lard. Drop dessertspoonfuls of the batter into the pan and cook on one side until bubbles begin to burst and they look dry. Turn and cook them on the other side. Reduce the heat during cooking if the griddle becomes too hot. When cooked, place in a tea towel to retain their soft texture while you cook the remainder.

Hot Cross Buns

[MAKES 12 BUNS]

We often used to serve fruit buns for staff teas. These days I find the new quick-mix yeasts easier than fresh yeast, but make sure you beat the yeast in well for a light bun. If you like a spicier bun, just add an extra pinch of cinnamon, nutmeg or cloves. They are best eaten on the day they are made.

1 lb (450 g) strong white flour

1 sachet easy-blend yeast

a pinch of salt

1 teaspoon ground mixed spice

2 oz (50 g) caster sugar

4 oz (100 g) currants

1 oz (25 g) chopped mixed peel

1 egg, beaten

8 fl oz (250 ml) milk

2 oz (50 g) butter, melted

FOR THE CROSSES:

4 tablespoons plain flour

a little water

beaten egg

FOR THE GLAZE:

2 oz (50 g) sugar

¼ pint (150 ml) water

Mix the flour, yeast, salt, spice, sugar, currants and mixed peel in a mixing bowl. Beat together the egg, milk and melted butter, then mix them into the dry ingredients and beat well to make a firm dough. When your hand comes away clean, the mixture is ready. Turn on to a lightly floured board and knead for about 5 minutes until smooth. Divide into 12 pieces and roll the buns to make the top smooth. Place them, well apart, on a greased baking tray, cover with an oiled plastic bag and put in a warm place for about 1 hour until doubled in size.

Pre-heat the oven to 425°F (220°C), gas mark 7. Put the flour for the crosses in a mixing bowl and add just enough water to make a very firm dough. Roll out to a long strand and cut into 24 × 2 in (5 cm) pieces. Brush the tops of the risen buns with beaten egg and fix two strands on each in a cross. Bake the buns for about 15 to 20 minutes until golden brown.

Meanwhile, dissolve the sugar in the water then boil it until reduced and syrupy. When the buns are cooked, brush over the glaze as soon as you take them out of the oven. Transfer them to a wire rack to cool.

SAUCES AND BASIC RECIPES

Basic White Sauce

[MAKES ½ PINT (300 ML)]

I consider this to be a 'base' sauce. Master this one and you can make caper, curry, parsley, mushroom or so many other sweet and savoury sauces. I always make white sauce by the traditional method of cooking the butter and flour first before adding the milk. The taste is not the same if it is made with the modern all-in-one method, and you really can't go wrong making it this way. If you are in a hurry, you can boil the milk first and the sauce is done in no time. I use a 'flat' whisk or sometimes a shaped spoon for sauce-making, or a bamboo whisk if I am making a large quantity. Of course, a drop of cream nearly always improves any sauce.

1 oz (25 g) unsalted butter

1 oz (25 g) plain flour

½ pint (300 ml) milk

salt and freshly ground black pepper

a little milk or single cream

Melt the butter in a saucepan, then remove from the heat and stir in the flour. Cook over a low heat, stirring continuously, for about 3 minutes. Stir in the milk a little at a time, bring back to the boil, season with salt and freshly ground black pepper and simmer, stirring, for about 3 minutes, mixing in a little milk or cream for the consistency you require.

SAVOURY VARIATIONS

CAPER SAUCE

1 tablespoon capers

Add these to the white sauce once it has boiled.

CELERY SAUCE

1 oz (25 g) unsalted butter

2 sticks celery, finely chopped

Melt the butter in a pan and gently fry the celery for about 4 minutes. Add to the white sauce once it has boiled.

CHEESE SAUCE

2 oz (50 g) mature Cheddar cheese, grated

½ teaspoon mustard powder

a pinch of cayenne pepper

Add the ingredients to the finished white sauce. Choose a strong cheese to give a good cheesy taste. I cannot bear to have something cheesy which does not taste of cheese! Don't put the sauce back on the heat once you have added the cheese otherwise it will go stringy.

CURRY SAUCE

2 teaspoons curry powder

Stir this into the butter and flour when making the white sauce and cook for 3 minutes, otherwise the curry powder will taste gritty or raw.

EGG SAUCE

2 hard-boiled eggs, chopped

Stir these into the white sauce once it has boiled.

HERB SAUCES

1 tablespoon chopped fresh dill, parsley, tarragon, etc.

I always fry my parsley in a little butter before adding it to the completed sauce, as sometimes it seems to make the sauce thin. I pour boiling water over other herbs, then remove them quickly. This keeps them a nice green and stops them tasting too strong. Just stir the prepared chopped herbs into the white sauce once it has boiled.

MUSHROOM SAUCE

1 oz (25 g) unsalted butter

4 oz (100 g) mushrooms, chopped

Melt the butter in a pan and gently fry the mushrooms for about 4 minutes. Add to the white sauce once it has boiled.

MUSTARD SAUCE

1 tablespoon made mustard

Stir the mustard to taste into the white sauce once it has boiled.

ONION SAUCE

1 oz (25 g) unsalted butter

1 onion, chopped

Melt the butter in a pan and gently fry the onions for about 5 minutes without letting them brown. Stir them into the white sauce once it has boiled. Alternatively, boil the chopped onion in a little water until soft. Use the water with an equal quantity of milk to make the white sauce and add the onion to the sauce once it has boiled.

The chopped onion gives a nice texture which goes well with roast leg of lamb.

SWEET VARIATION

1 tablespoon sugar

1 × 1 in (2.5 cm) piece of vanilla pod

grated rind of 1 lemon

Before making the white sauce, bring the milk to the boil with the sugar, vanilla and lemon rind and leave it to infuse for 30 minutes. Strain and use to make a white sauce.

Béchamel Sauce

[MAKES ½ PINT (300 ML)]

½ *pint (300 ml) milk*

---

1 medium carrot, grated

---

2 sticks celery, chopped

---

1 small onion, grated

---

2 cloves

---

6 peppercorns

---

1 oz (25 g) unsalted butter

---

1 oz (25 g) plain flour

---

a pinch of salt

1–2 tablespoons cream

Put the milk, carrot, celery, onion, cloves and peppercorns in a saucepan and bring almost to boiling point. Remove from the heat and leave to infuse for 30 minutes. Strain the milk, pressing the vegetables well to extract all the milk. Discard the vegetables. Melt the butter in a saucepan and add the flour. Cook without browning for about 1 minute. Gradually add the seasoned milk and boil for 3 minutes, stirring continuously. Season with salt and stir in the cream.

Hollandaise Sauce

[MAKES ½ PINT (300 ML)]

If you want to make this sauce lighter, whisk up the white of an egg and whisk it in just before serving. I used to save any sauce that came back from the dining room and add a little cream to it the next day to make the salad dressing. Today I use fromage frais. If you find the sauce too sharp with wine vinegar, use a little lemon juice instead.

---

3 tablespoons white wine vinegar or lemon juice to taste

---

6 peppercorns

---

1 small bay leaf

---

2 egg yolks

4–6 oz (100–175 g) unsalted butter, softened

---

salt and freshly ground white pepper

Put the vinegar or lemon juice, peppercorns and bay leaf in a saucepan, bring to the boil and boil until reduced to 1 tablespoonful. Put the egg yolks in a bowl over a pan of hot water, add the strained vinegar and stir with a wooden spoon or small whisk until the yolks thicken, then gradually work in the butter in small pieces. Do not allow the water to boil; remove it from the heat if it gets too hot. Season to taste with salt and freshly ground white pepper and serve warm.

Quick Hollandaise Sauce

[MAKES ½ PINT (300 ML)]

This recipe came from a collection made by several ladies and sold in aid of the Red Cross in 1982–3. It is a good quick recipe, but not in the same class as the 'slow' method. I still use the pepper mill, but use white peppercorns for this; once you've got into the habit of grinding pepper it's hard to accept the powder.

---

4 egg yolks

---

juice of 1 lemon

---

8 oz (225 g) unsalted butter

---

salt and freshly ground white pepper

Put the egg yolks in the food processor and process for a few seconds. While the processor is still running, add the lemon juice. Melt the butter and bring it almost to boiling point. Then, with the processor running, gradually pour it into the egg yolks in a steady stream. Blend for a further minute. Season to taste with salt and freshly ground white pepper. Keep the sauce warm until ready to serve.

Velouté Sauce

[MAKES ½ PINT (300 ML)]

---

1 oz (25 g) unsalted butter

---

1 oz (25 g) plain flour

---

1 pint (600 ml) Chicken Stock (see page 198) or veal stock, hot

---

salt and freshly ground black pepper

---

2 tablespoons double cream

Melt the butter in a saucepan. Stir in the flour, then gradually stir in the hot stock, making sure the sauce remains smooth. Simmer for about 45 minutes, stirring occasionally, or until the sauce is reduced by half. Strain, season to taste with salt and freshly ground black pepper and stir in the cream.

Tartare Sauce

[MAKES ¼ PINT (150 ML)]

Home-made Tartare Sauce is so much nicer than bottled – and so easy!

¼ pint (150 ml) Creamy Mayonnaise (see page 197)

---

1 teaspoon chopped gherkins

---

1 teaspoon chopped capers

---

1 teaspoon chopped fresh parsley

½ teaspoon chopped fresh chervil

½ teaspoon chopped fresh tarragon

Mix all the ingredients together.

French Dressing

[MAKES ½ PINT (300 ML)]

I vary my salad dressings to suit what I am serving; I tend just to hurtle things in! I think French Dressing tastes better if it is not too sharp, and I use a little more oil than some recipes.

1 teaspoon made mustard

a pinch of caster sugar

8 fl oz (250 ml) olive oil

2 fl oz (50 ml) white wine vinegar, tarragon vinegar or lemon juice, or to taste

a few drops of Worcestershire sauce

1 teaspoon chopped fresh chives, mint or parsley (optional)

Mix all the ingredients together well. Mix again before serving.

Admiral's Dressing

[MAKES ABOUT ½ PINT (300 ML)]

This is a useful salad dressing which I make up in a bottle; it keeps in the fridge for ages. You can add a chopped clove of garlic if you wish.

4 tablespoons sugar

4 tablespoons Worcestershire sauce

4 tablespoons tomato ketchup

4 tablespoons white wine vinegar

8 fl oz (250 ml) olive oil

1 teaspoon salt

2 shallots, finely chopped

juice of 1–2 lemons

Mix all the ingredients together well, adding lemon juice to taste. Store in an airtight bottle in the fridge and shake well before using.

Creamy Mayonnaise

[MAKES ½ PINT (300 ML)]

I prefer 'hand-made' mayonnaise, but an electric hand whisk is fine. I'm naughty again, adding the oil straight from the bottle tucked under my arm, with a slit cut into the cork, the way 'old chef' taught me! I use a wine vinegar, so choose one to suit your taste, and I sometimes add a little cream before using the mayonnaise if I am making it for an egg dish.

½ pint (300 ml) olive oil

2 egg yolks

a pinch of salt

1 teaspoon made mustard

3 tablespoons white wine vinegar, tarragon vinegar or lemon juice, or to taste

Measure the oil into a jug that pours well. Put the egg yolks in a basin with the salt and mustard and whisk well until the yolks are thick. Now add the oil, drop by drop, whisking all the time, until the mixture begins to thicken. When it begins to get a shiny look, add the oil a little faster. Mix in the vinegar or lemon juice to taste.

Clarified Butter

[MAKES 8 OZ (225 G)]

I generally use unsalted butter which does not need clarifying; but if you clarify salted butter it is better to cook with as it doesn't burn so quickly in the pan.

1 lb (450 g) butter

½ pint (300 ml) boiling water

Melt the butter in a saucepan. Bring it almost to boiling point, then remove from the heat and add the boiling water. Be careful as it will spit. The impurities will sink to the bottom. Leave it to solidify, then lift out the butter in one piece and it is ready for use. You will need to scrape off the milky residue.

Chicken Stock

[Makes about 1 pint (600 ml)]

You can always use a good proprietary brand of stock cube for your soups; in fact I sometimes add a stock cube when I am making stock to give it extra flavour. But if you want to get the most out of your chicken carcass, you can make your own stock. I often use the slo-cooker, which can be left overnight to look after itself. All the ingredients are approximate, as you can vary the vegetables according to what you have in the cupboard. If you are going to freeze the finished stock, reduce it by boiling for about 20 minutes, then it takes up less space. I find it handy to keep some stock in the freezer as I prefer to make soups from fresh ingredients rather than freezing finished soups.

1 chicken carcass

1 large onion, quartered

4 oz (100 g) carrots, sliced

1–2 sticks celery, sliced

1–2 leeks, sliced

1 bouquet garni

½ teaspoon salt

6 peppercorns

1 chicken stock cube (optional)

Place all the ingredients in a large saucepan and cover with cold water. Bring to the boil, then cover and simmer on the lowest heat for about 3 hours to extract all the flavour. Strain the stock and allow it to cool. Skim any fat off the surface by drawing a piece of kitchen paper across it. Reduce, if required, by boiling for a further 20 minutes.

Fish Stock

[MAKES ½ PINT (300 ML)]

I like to make stock to use for any fish sauces. Sole bones are the best if you can get them, but you can use any fish bones.

8 oz (225 g) sole bones
1 onion, quartered
1 bay leaf

Put the ingredients in a saucepan and cover with cold water. Bring to the boil and add 2 spoonfuls of cold water. This will make the scum rise to the top. Skim this off, bring the water back to the boil and simmer for about 45 minutes, skimming again if necessary. Strain. This should make a nice clear stock.

Shortcrust Pastry

[MAKES 8 OZ (225 G)]

I always make my pastry by hand; if you use a knife or a mixer you don't have the same feel of how the pastry is working. I always keep a milk bottle full of water in the fridge so that I have ice cold water ready to make pastry.

8 oz (225 g) plain flour
a pinch of salt
2½ oz (65 g) unsalted butter
2½ oz (65 g) lard
2–3 tablespoons ice cold water

Put the flour and salt in a mixing bowl and rub in the fat until the mixture resembles fine breadcrumbs. Gradually add the ice cold water until the pastry binds together.

Easy Flaky Pastry

[MAKES 6 OZ (175 G)]

My mother used to make the most lovely flaky pastry, but then we used to be able to buy 'real lard'. There was a good pork butcher's in Newbury and they had big enamel pans of lard on market days; cold and crinkly on the top. Mum used to buy some and we'd come home and have bread and lard for tea with brown sugar on the top. It sounds funny today, but it was delicious. I can see my mum now; she used to stand in the kitchen, rolling out the pastry and plopping the lard in in bits, then bake it in the old coal oven.

We also used to buy bladders of lard for the big houses: a pig's bladder filled with lard that we used to slice off. That was more expensive than ordinary lard, though, so it was kept for the dining room.

Put the margarine in the freezer for 25 minutes before starting. Sift the flour and salt into a large mixing bowl and take out enough flour into a small bowl to use for dipping. Using a piece of kitchen foil, grip the frozen margarine and grate it into the bowl on the large side of the grater. Cover the surface of the flour with fat. When the margarine becomes sticky, dip it into the small bowl of flour. Finally tip the remaining flour into the mixing bowl. Cut and mix the margarine into the flour, then add enough ice cold water to make a firm dough. At the last minute, when the mixture is crumbly, use your hands to mix it gently into a ball. Wrap the pastry in foil or put it in a polythene bag and chill it for at least 30 minutes before using.

6 oz (175 g) hard margarine

8 oz (225 g) plain flour

a pinch of salt

ice cold water

John Tovey's Easy Puff Pastry

[Makes 1 lb (450 g)]

1 lb (450 g) strong plain flour

a generous pinch of salt

8 oz (225 g) soft margarine

8 oz (225 g) soft vegetable lard

1 tablespoon lemon juice made up to $\frac{1}{2}$ pint (300 ml) with ice cold water

Sieve the flour and salt into a mixing bowl. Scatter over walnut-sized lumps of margarine and lard and coat them gently in the flour. Make a hollow in the middle, pour in the liquid and use a palette knife to form the mixture into a rough dough. Turn it on to a well floured surface and shape it gently into a brick. With a rolling pin, make 3 indentations across the top of the brick. Sprinkle with flour if lots of fat is visible. Rest the rolling pin in the middle indentation and carefully roll the top of the brick away from you. Repeat from the bottom indentation to the middle, making a perfect rectangle after each roll. Square off the corners. Fold the bottom third up away from you and the top third down on top of this. Press down with the rolling pin on 3 sides. Leave the pastry to rest for 5 minutes.

Repeat the process of rolling and folding the pastry 3 times, leaving the pastry to rest for 5 minutes between each rolling. Make sure you do not stretch the pastry. After the fourth turn, the dough should be light and springy. If you want to use the pastry straight away, chill it, then allow it to return to room temperature before using. Alternatively, you can wrap the pastry in plastic and put it in the freezer.

Butterscotch Sauce

[MAKES ABOUT $\frac{1}{2}$ PINT (300 ML)]

You can serve this sauce with puddings and ice-cream. It keeps well in the fridge.

1 egg yolk

4 oz (100 g) unsalted butter

4 oz (100 g) soft light brown sugar

3 fl oz (85 ml) golden syrup

a squeeze of lemon juice

2 fl oz (50 ml) water

1 tablespoon cream

Beat the egg yolk, then mix in the butter, sugar, syrup, lemon juice and water. Cook in a double saucepan or in a bowl over hot water until the sauce becomes a thick syrup. Stir in the cream. Serve hot or cold.

Lemon Syrup Sauce

[MAKES ABOUT $\frac{1}{2}$ PINT (300 ML)]

6 oz (175 g) caster sugar

2 tablespoons golden syrup

$\frac{1}{4}$ pint (150 ml) water

1 oz (25 g) unsalted butter

a squeeze of lemon juice, or to taste

Put the sugar, syrup and water in a small saucepan, bring to the boil and simmer for about 5 minutes. Remove from the heat and stir in the butter and lemon juice.

Chocolate Sauce

[MAKES ABOUT $\frac{1}{2}$ PINT (300 ML)]

I prefer to use a vanilla pod instead of vanilla essence; it is very easy to use and much better, so have a pot of sugar and put a vanilla pod in. If you do use the essence, be careful – better too little than too much.

3 oz (75 g) plain or milk chocolate, broken into pieces

2 oz (50 g) caster sugar

1 teaspoon cocoa

$\frac{1}{2}$ pint (300 ml) water

a small piece of vanilla pod or 2 drops of vanilla essence

1 egg yolk

Put the chocolate, sugar, cocoa and half the water in a saucepan. Stir over a low heat until the chocolate has melted and the mixture is boiling. Simmer for 2 to 3 minutes, then add the rest of the water and the vanilla pod or essence. Bring back to the boil, then simmer gently for about 10 minutes until the sauce looks nice and syrupy. Remove from the heat and mix about 2 tablespoons of the sauce into the egg yolk. Stir well, then return this mixture to the saucepan and mix well. This way you will find your sauce is less likely to curdle the egg.

Ruth's Cream Fudge

[MAKES ABOUT 30 SWEETS]

This is an easy method of making fudge and takes about 20 minutes from start to finish, but you will have to stay with it and stir as it catches very easily. If you do not have a thermometer, drop a little fudge into cold water. If it forms a soft ball between finger and thumb, grab it off the stove quickly and start beating!

---

4 oz (100 g) unsalted butter

---

1 × 14 oz (400 g) tin full-cream sweetened condensed milk

---

1 lb (450 g) demerara sugar

Melt the butter and condensed milk together, add the demerara sugar and cook until the mixture begins to candy. This should be at about 239°F (115°C). Remove from the heat and beat very well. Pour into a buttered tin and cut into squares before it gets cold.

Coconut Ice

[MAKES ABOUT 20 BARS]

This recipe comes from a *Good Housekeeping* book which I bought before the War in 1939 for 1 shilling! It has been invaluable to me over the years for WI stalls and fêtes. I like my coconut fairly coarse, but the choice is yours. If you want two colours, make two separate batches and colour them with a few drops of food colouring.

---

2 lb (1 kg) loaf or granulated sugar

½ pint (300 ml) cold water

---

8 oz (225 g) desiccated coconut

Dissolve the sugar in the water in a saucepan, then bring the mixture to the boil until it reaches 239°F (115°C) or when a spoonful forms a soft ball when dropped in cold water. Remove from the heat and add the coconut. Stir until thick and pour into an oiled or wetted tin. Cut into bars when cool.

Barley Water

[MAKES 2 PINTS (1.2 LITRES)]

This recipe makes a lovely, smooth drink. I used to make it every day for use in the nursery or sick room. To add a little extra flavour, you can stir in a small piece of lemon peel after it has been sweetened, or you can add it to simmer with the barley.

2 oz (50 g) pearl barley, washed

1 pint (600 ml) cold water

4 pints (2.25 litres) boiling water

sugar to taste

juice of 1 lemon

Put the pearl barley in a saucepan with the cold water, bring to the boil and simmer for 15 minutes. Strain off the water and add the 4 pints (2.25 litres) of boiling water. Continue boiling until the liquid has reduced by half. Strain into a cool jug, stir in sugar and lemon juice to taste and it is ready to serve.

Claret Cup

[MAKES 2 PINTS (1.2 LITRES)]

This makes a refreshing summer cup for a lunchtime party.

2 glasses dry sherry

a little grated nutmeg

8 cloves

2 tablespoons caster sugar

juice and rind of $\frac{1}{2}$ small lemon

6 leaves of mint
or 2 slices cucumber
or a sprig of borage

1 × 75 cl bottle claret

$\frac{1}{2}$ pint (300 ml) soda water

Put the sherry, nutmeg, cloves, sugar, lemon rind and juice and mint, cucumber or borage in a 2 pint (1.2 litre) jug. Stir in $\frac{1}{4}$ pint (150 ml) of claret and leave to stand for 20 minutes. Then remove the cloves, lemon rind and mint, cucumber or borage. Immediately before serving, add the soda water and the remaining claret.

Ginger Wine

[MAKES ABOUT 1 GALLON (4.5 LITRES)]

We used to make wine from all sorts of things. In fact, when I was a girl everyone in the village would make their own wine and taste each other's. Ours was kept in an old earthenware bread crock outside the back door until strained and bottled, with a slice of toast spread with yeast floating on the top. We used to have to stir it every day, and when you lifted the lid, the little black flies used to come out in all directions! But no one came to any harm. We are so used to everything clean these days, we've gone too far the other way.

My brother once came off worse for some home-made beetroot wine. He had gone to celebrate a friend's bachelor night party and came back home through the wood. But he could not find his way along the path so he groped his way into the field so he would know where he was. Unfortunately, he couldn't find the gate to get out again, so he didn't come home till morning!

---

1 lb (450 g) raisins, chopped

1½ oz (40 g) dried root ginger, bruised

3½ lb (1.5 kg) granulated or demerara sugar

1½ gallons (6.75 litres) water

---

juice of 2 lemons

---

1 oz (25 g) fresh yeast

Put the raisins in a wine crock or fermentation bucket. Put the ginger, sugar and water in a large saucepan, bring to the boil and simmer for 30 minutes. Pour over the raisins and add the lemon juice. When the mixture is lukewarm, stir in the fresh yeast. Cover and leave for 2 weeks, stirring every day, then siphon into bottles, leaving the tops not quite closed. When the yeast stops working – the bubbles stop coming out of the top of the bottle – begin to tighten the bottle a little more each day until sealed.

We did not buy alcoholic drinks in the old days. The cottagers would make their own, and perhaps have a glass of port for a really special occasion, or some home-made sloe gin. Later, when my mother was ill and I called on her on a winter morning when it was frosty, I used to put a tablespoon of whisky in her tea. She used to sniff it and say, 'It smells a bit like tea this morning!'

As a young woman, she had been the only woman who climbed up the church steeple from the outside! When they were putting a new top on, she climbed up the ladder to view the village. The old people used to talk about it years later.

INDEX

Italic page numbers indicate a colour illustration